MW01093930

Draw Close to Jesus

Draw Close to
JESUS

A Woman's Guide to
EUCHARISTIC ADORATION

Merridith Frediani

Our Sunday Visitor
Huntington, Indiana

Nihil Obstat
Msgr. Michael Heintz, Ph.D.
Censor Librorum

Imprimatur
✠ Kevin C. Rhoades
Bishop of Fort Wayne-South Bend
April 14, 2021

The *Nihil Obstat* and *Imprimatur* are official declarations that a book is free from doctrinal or moral error. It is not implied that those who have granted the *Nihil Obstat* and *Imprimatur* agree with the contents, opinions, or statements expressed.

Our Sunday Visitor Publishing Division, Our Sunday Visitor, Inc., 200 Noll Plaza, Huntington, IN 46750; www.osv.com; 1-800-348-2440

ISBN: 978-1-68192-594-3 (Inventory No. T2458)

1. RELIGION—Christianity—Catholic.
2. RELIGION—Christian Life—Women's Issues.
3. RELIGION—Christian Life—Spiritual Growth.

LCCN: 2021936252

Cover design and Interior design: Amanda Falk
Cover art: AdobeStock

PRINTED IN THE UNITED STATES OF AMERICA

I dedicate this book to the Blessed Virgin
Mary — the greatest woman ever — who
always points us toward her Son.

To the Frediani FamBam: the three people God allowed
me to be the mother of so that I could experience
the physicality and emotionality of womanhood,
and to my husband, Rob, who in his manhood
is my perfect complement and best friend.

Finally, to my friend Dan, who with a sly grin and a twinkle
in his eye made me laugh so hard I fell over. I miss you.

Finally, brethren, whatever is true, whatever is honorable,
whatever is just, whatever is pure, whatever is lovely,
whatever is gracious, if there is any excellence, if there
is anything worthy of praise, think about these things.
What you have learned and received and heard and
seen in me, do; and the God of peace will be with you.

Philippians 4:8–9

Contents

∼

∼

Introduction

This is a book for women.

God created two ways of being human — man and woman — and while we are all rightly classified as *Homo sapiens*, we are different, and those differences go beyond our chromosomes and physical attributes. They go as deep as our souls.

Women and men express humanity in distinct ways: how we think, love, relate to others, and function. We are equal in dignity, but we are not the same. In our differences we complement and enhance each other, and humankind is better for it.

In her lyrical book *These Beautiful Bones*, Emily Stimpson Chapman describes the tasks of women as spiritual motherhood. As women we receive the gift of all the people God sends us, we welcome them, we show them hospitality. We are attentive when we pause to talk and listen to those we encounter. We cultivate gentleness in controlling our strength and considering how others will hear what we say, and we are advocates, reminding others of their beauty and worth. These tasks "don't require a lot of time but (they) do require a lot of us."

In adoration we approach God as women and pause in these tasks to acknowledge that God calls to us in the deep core of our hearts. He wants us to come to him and rest. We do not need to bring anything. He knows the world is pulling at us and can be overwhelming. He knows we make mistakes, and he keeps inviting. When we come to him, we open ourselves to the one who loves us most deeply. We bring him our empty vessel, and he fills it. We sit in adoration of him, and he receives us as gifts, he listens, and he reminds us of our beauty and worth. He loves us wholly and completely, for no other reason than that we exist, and we are his.

During his earthly ministry, Jesus counted several women among his followers: the Virgin Mary, Mary and Martha, Mary Magdalene, and many others. He also encountered, forgave, and healed women (the woman at the well, the hemorrhaging woman, the woman caught in adultery). These were women whose lives were changed after their time with Jesus. Our lives too are changed when we spend time with Jesus in Eucharistic adoration.

This book is an invitation for women to build a habit of Eucharistic adoration. My hope is that you will fall in love with Jesus through spending time with him. This book includes reflections and encouragement. The reflections cover a variety of topics, so feel free to skip around and go to whichever one is speaking to you. This book will help you slow down, be still, and know that God is with you in a real way. An enriching prayer life, like any great friendship, requires that both people talk and both listen. This book is designed to help you not only speak to God but also develop a disposition to hear God speaking. I also hope that it will give you encouragement to keep praying even in times of dryness.

In this book you will find snippets from saints and quotes from Sacred Scripture and the *Catechism of the Catholic Church* to frame the reflections. There is also a section on some well-known devotions for those days when you need other people's words, ancient words that connect us to the Body of Christ.

Please join me in growing closer to the Lord who is so in love with us. I am confident that if you accept Christ's invitation to meet him in adoration, he will do amazing things in your heart.

Part I
Adoration How-To

I f you have never attended Eucharistic adoration and you're not sure what to do or expect, read on. This first section, which I've set up as an adoration primer, is especially for you. Even if you're an adoration pro, I encourage you not to skip this section. It never hurts to get back to the basics.

When you enter the chapel or church where adoration is happening, you will notice a few things. The Blessed Sacrament (the Host) is in a monstrance on the altar. The monstrance is a vessel that contains a clear section that allows us to see the Host. There are candles on both sides of the monstrance. Often the lights are dimmed, and there is a sense of peace.

Before you enter your pew or sit down, be sure to genuflect if you can. (If you are unable to genuflect, you may make a reverent bow.) The Blessed Sacrament is the Real Presence of Jesus — not a symbol. He is there! And it is important to show him reverence.

Often people begin their time in adoration kneeling. Some stay kneeling the whole time; others sit. Do what feels comfortable for you. There is no right or wrong.

If you are in the church for the Exposition of the Sacrament — in other words, when Jesus is placed in the monstrance — you will kneel with the congregation as he is processed to the altar. After the monstrance is set on the altar, you will likely sing the hymn "*O Salutaris Hostia*":

O salutaris Hostia *Quae caeli pandis ostium:* *Bella premunt hostilia,* *Da robur, fer auxilium.*	O saving Victim, open wide The gate of heaven to us below, Our foes press on from every side; Your aid supply, your strength bestow.
Uni trinoque Domino *Sit sempiterna gloria,* *Qui vitam sine termino* *Nobis donet in patria. Amen.*	To your great name be endless praise, Immortal Godhead, One in Three; O grant us endless length of days In our true native land to be. Amen.

How you spend your time in adoration is up to you. Some people pray in their own words. You may want to pray a Rosary, write in a journal, or read the Bible. The reflections in this book are meant to be read and prayed with while you are in adoration to help you organize your time and develop a habit of prayer. I also encourage you to check out the "Catholic Stuff" section of this book, where you will find other prayers you can pray as well.

The amount of time you spend in adoration is also up to you. Some people stay for an hour; some stay less. You may find in the beginning that ten or fifteen minutes is plenty, and as you attend adoration more, you will stay longer. Like many good things, spending time in adoration takes some practice. Be patient with yourself. It will come.

The Benediction takes place when the time of adoration is over, before the Blessed Sacrament is replaced in the tabernacle. If you are present, you may witness several things.

First, the faithful will likely sing the hymn *"Tantum Ergo"*:

Tantum ergo Sacramentum	Down in adoration falling,
Veneremur cernui,	Lo! The sacred Host we hail;
Et antiquum documentum	Lo! O'er ancient forms departing,
Novo cedat ritui;	Newer rites of grace prevail;
Praestet fides supplementum,	Faith for all defects supplying,
Sensuum defectui.	Where the feeble senses fail.
Genitori Genitoque	To the everlasting Father,
Laus et jubilatio,	And the Son who reigns on high,
Salus, honor, virtue quoque	With the Holy Spirit proceeding
Sit et benedictio:	Forth from each eternally,
Procedenti ab utroque.	Be salvation, honor, blessing,
Compar sit laudatio. Amen.	Might and endless majesty. Amen.

The priest will then bless the congregation with the monstrance and lead the Divine Praises:

> Blessed be God.
> Blessed be his Holy Name.
> Blessed be Jesus Christ, true God and true Man.
> Blessed be the Name of Jesus.
> Blessed be his most Sacred Heart.
> Blessed be his most Precious Blood.
> Blessed be Jesus in the most Holy Sacrament of the Altar.
> Blessed be the Holy Spirit, the Paraclete.
> Blessed be the great Mother of God, Mary most holy.
> Blessed be her holy and Immaculate Conception.
> Blessed be her glorious Assumption.
> Blessed be the name of Mary, Virgin and Mother.
> Blessed be St. Joseph, her most chaste spouse.
> Blessed be God in his angels and in his saints.

Jesus is then returned to the tabernacle, and it is common for the faithful to then sing "Holy God, We Praise Thy Name" to end the time in adoration:

Holy God we praise thy name,
Lord of all we bow before thee
All on earth thy scepter claim,
All in heaven above adore thee
Infinite thy vast domain,
Everlasting is thy reign.

To do: Before you leave adoration, even if you are not present for Benediction, pray the Divine Praises.

To go deeper: Pray with the words of "*O Salutaris Hostia*," "*Tantum Ergo*," or "Holy God, We Praise Thy Name." Read through the hymn slowly, pausing at each line.

Beginning

And the rib which the Lord God had taken
from the man he made into a woman.

Genesis 2:22

In Genesis, we read of the start of all that is. We are starting our own beginning right now. We are beginning a regular practice of Eucharistic adoration.

We know our heavenly Father desires us to be in communion with him through his Son, Jesus. All of us have a God-shaped hole in our heart, and until it is filled, we are, as Saint Augustine said, restless. When he created everything from nothing, God chose to create each one of us. He knit us together in our mother's womb (see Ps 139). We are made intentionally, not accidentally. We are here for a reason, and we are assured it is good.

God created us to desire him, to need him, to be fulfilled only by him. He calls us. Each of us hears this call differently. Some feel gentle stirrings, others hear clear commands. Sometimes we are not sure whether we are called, but faith tells us we are. We are called to be in relationship with our God. As women we tend toward reflecting and feeling. We are often caregivers to children or parents. We love by serving and sacrificing. We offer comfort. We are present. Our relationship with God flips that around. Jesus sacrificed for us. Jesus is present to us and offers us comfort. Jesus gives us the things we offer others, and the more we come to him, the better we will be able to love those he places in our lives.

In adoration, we are still and silent — something that is hard to do in a noisy world. But that is when God comes to us. He doesn't roar; he whispers. With time we will become better at hearing his quiet voice.

Let us take this time to grow closer to him. Let us be intentional about it. Go to the websites of churches near you to find out when they offer adoration. You may even have a church in your area that offers perpetual adoration, which means Jesus is always in the monstrance and available for you to make a visit. If you live near a university, check the Newman Center, as they may have weekly adoration.

To do: Consider your weekly and daily schedule. Take it in pieces. Look at the next four weeks and mark on your calendar when you will commit to going to adoration. Don't look any further right now. Just tackle the first four weeks. When that is over, schedule the next four.

To go deeper: Consecrate this time to Jesus. Give him your concerns about this new practice and tell him what is exciting about it for you. Ask him to give you the grace you need to meet him more deeply. Remind yourself of his great love for you.

Endurance

I can do all things in him who strengthens me.

Philippians 4:13

Eucharistic adoration is very easy and, paradoxically, rather hard. It requires us to use one of our most limited commodities — time — on something that at first may seem to be nothing more than sitting around.

We may approach adoration with excitement: *This will be a time of peace in my nutty life. I've heard good things come from this devotion.* Or we may feel it is something we should do, but we aren't quite sure we want to (and then we feel guilty). The first few weeks might be great, but then life creeps in and we stop going.

Making a regular habit of Eucharistic adoration is kind of like making a habit of exercise. At first your hopes are high, you are excited about the benefits, and you carve out the time. You push through the initial challenge — the sore muscles, the tiredness — and you feel great. You resolve never to stop this wonderful new habit. Then it gets hard, or your schedule becomes less accommodating, and you do it less often. If you aren't careful, over time you will exercise less and less because although you feel great when you exercise and you enjoy it, you feel selfish for taking that time for yourself. Then you realize that when you go back, it is going to be hard again, and that all your work has worn off. It's no use, you tell yourself. Your well-intentioned plan falls apart. Let's have a cookie.

Yet, if you stick with it, if you push through that challenging part, if you return even after an absence, exercise can become a part of you. The same is true of prayer in Eucharistic adoration. The more you persist, even when you fail, the more you learn that your hard work is not lost. You stop judging yourself as you learn that Jesus is always waiting patiently and is happy to welcome you back. You realize that taking this time isn't selfish — it's necessary. You become better when you spend time with Jesus. You develop a more peaceful soul. And as you form the habit, if you miss your regular adoration time, you feel it.

Spending time in the Real Presence of Our Lord is powerful. It is a guarantee that your life will change. God is not a trickster. He desires you to come to him, and he doesn't hold back his graces. He also knows the temptations that pull you away, such as feeling unworthy because of your sin, desiring perfection and not being patient with yourself as you grow. You may feel selfish because you are taking time for yourself instead of caring for your children, your elderly parent, or your sick friend. You may feel frustrated because nothing seems to be happening as you sit in adoration.

But something is happening. You may not feel the feelings you expect, but deep in your soul God is working. This is the time for endurance. You can do all things in him who strengthens you.

To do: What specifically in your life is going to challenge your commitment to adoration? Share this with Jesus and ask for help.

To go deeper: Ask Jesus what he wants from you during this time. Ask him to reveal his will for your life and for the courage to surrender to it.

Mindset ... Heartset

Take my yoke upon you and learn from me; for I am gentle and lowly in heart, and you will find rest for your souls. For my yoke is easy, and my burden is light.

Matthew 11:29–30

When I go to adoration, I bring the "me" of that day. Some days I am happy and peaceful. Other days I am dark and stormy. The blessing is that Jesus wants us near him every day. We are invited to bring him whatever we are. We are encouraged to be real in his Real Presence.

Sometimes we go to him in adoration with our minds racing or our hearts unsettled. The worries of the day are a bulky backpack. It's hard to stop the scattered scurrying of concerns through our head.

Jesus says to us: *Why do you carry such a heavy stone? Lay it down. Lay your burden down and carry my yoke instead. I will give you rest.*

In adoration, we learn to do as he asks. We sit at Jesus' feet and learn how we can drop our worries and leave them for him, carrying instead the yoke he offers. And in those times when it feels like the burden is too heavy, when our hearts are sad and our minds overwhelmed and we collapse under the weight, he carries us.

It is easy to say, "I want to let go of this load," but it is not easy to do. I have realized that if I try to do it on my own, I cannot. The trouble keeps surfacing and causing me unrest. I must ask Jesus for help. He can help me stop worrying. He slows down the mental hamster wheel.

When I first started attending Eucharistic adoration, I felt like I spent the whole visit striving after an unattainable inner quiet. I imagined myself sitting by a river next to Jesus on a summer day. Barges filled with my aggravations would float past while I tried to push them away, wishing for a quiet river. It was a lesson in futility, because even though Jesus was present, I wasn't letting him help. I was convinced that in order to be worthy of being with him, I had to first clear the river.

I slowly realized that was not how it works. The open heart and quiet mind I so desired were being offered free of charge. The barges of my hang-ups could continue to float past; I just had to stop watching them and watch Jesus instead. The junk in our life is always going to be there, but so is Jesus, and paying attention to him is far more satisfying.

To do: Use your imagination to place yourself somewhere with Jesus. Ask him to help you ignore the clutter and distractions of your life during this time with him, trusting that he will help you deal with it when the time comes.

To go deeper: Reread the Scripture verse at the beginning of this reflection (see Mt 11:29–30) and reflect on what Jesus wants you to hear.

Listening

Be still, and know that I am God.

Psalm 46:11

Some lucky people can sit in adoration, gazing on the Lord. They appear enraptured listening intently *and* hearing something. This is a grace I have not received. When I go to adoration, the first thing I have to do is slow down the monkey parade gamboling through my brain. Some days it feels impossible. My life is intrusive and won't let me step away. The plates I am carefully balancing threaten to crash to the floor, causing me to expend more precious mental energy. It is a spiritual circus with me at the center. I am Martha, of Martha and Mary's fame, worrying about cleaning my house and being prepared because Jesus is visiting, and everything has to be ready.

In adoration, though, we need to emulate Martha's sister, Mary, who sat at Christ's feet and listened. She wasn't worried about the details; she knew the best use of her time was to be in his presence and soak him in.

Just be. Just breathe. Just listen. That is the only thing he asks of us: Be with me.

Plenty of places in Scripture tell us to listen. We are assured that as Jesus' sheep, we will hear his voice. We are blessed if we hear the word of God and keep it. At the wedding in Cana, Mary directs the servants (us) to "do whatever he tells you" (Jn 2:5), but first we need to hear what he is saying. And because God speaks quietly, we are back to swatting the mosquitos buzzing in our ears.

So how do we listen for God in adoration?

1. Ask for God's grace to cultivate the ability to be still and listen.
2. Patiently wait for that grace.
3. Understand that the experience of listening is different for each of us.

Those people who can sit quietly in adoration smiling at Jesus are real, and that is their blessing. My blessing requires keeping part of my mind active so that the other part can receive. I've found the Rosary is perfect for that. Some find journaling a helpful way to aid the listening process. Others repeat a word or phrase. We are all different people, and we all use different methods to connect with God. Know that he will help you when you ask. Keep showing up to adoration and wait patiently for his help.

To do: Talk to Jesus as your friend and ask him to teach you to hear him. Ask him to help you identify your special way.

To go deeper: Read Psalm 46 and reflect on what it means to know that God is God.

Bringing My Real Self

O LORD, you have searched me and known me!
You know when I sit down and when I rise up;
you discern my thoughts from afar.

Psalm 139:1–2

"Here I am." These are three small yet powerful words.

Before Abraham was put to the test with Isaac, the Lord called him, and he responded, "Here I am" (Gn 22:1).

When God sent an angel to Jacob, he replied, "Here I am" (Gn 31:11).

God called out to Moses from the burning bush, and Moses answered, "Here I am" (Ex 3:4).

God called Samuel while he slept, and he answered, "Here I am" (1 Sm 3:4).

The Lord asked whom he should send, and Isaiah said, "Here I am" (Is 6:8).

The Lord sent Ananias to Saul, and Ananias responded, "Here I am" (Acts 9:10).

In our life with Christ, each day is an opportunity to say to Jesus once again, "Here I am."

God knows how much of a disaster we can be. Yet he keeps inviting, and his invitation isn't black tie — it's come as you are. If we waited until we were good enough, we would never arrive at his feet. We remind ourselves of this at every Mass when we pray, *Lord, I am not worthy that you should enter under my roof, but only say the word and my soul shall be healed.*

Jesus invites us in our spiritual sloppiness to come to him and simply say, "Here I am." He invites us to bring our real selves — the self that is judgmental, selfish, hurt, angry, sad, disappointed, or insert-your-own-emotion-here. We don't have to play our "A game" with Jesus. We don't have to be on our best, most polite behavior. We should be respectful, of course — he *is* the Lord of the Universe — but we can also be honest. We cannot hide who we are from him. He knows us better than we do. And still, he keeps calling. Some of my best experiences in adoration have been when I crack open that vault of ugly. I have felt him lift it from my heart and leave me with peace.

God is our loving Father. He doesn't want us to suffer. He loves us without condition, without price. We cannot earn it. We are not worthy. We can come to him and offer ourselves and our lives with the confidence that he will accept them. What a beautiful gift from our Creator — to go to him in prayer and simply say, "Here I am," confident we will be loved and accepted.

To do: Repeat "Here I am, Lord" over and over to help quiet your mind and heart. Offer to Jesus who you are today, knowing of his love for you. Ask him for help accepting this gift of love.

To go deeper: Pray with Psalm 139.

The Real Presence

I am the bread of life; he who comes
to me shall never hunger.

John 6:35

Imagine you are one of Jesus' followers hearing what we now call the Bread of Life discourse. Yesterday he fed five thousand men with just five loaves of bread and two fish. Today he is talking about bread again. You hear Jesus say, "I am the bread of life; he who comes to me shall not hunger, and he who believes in me shall never thirst" (Jn 6:35) and later "He who eats my flesh and drinks my blood has eternal life, and I will raise him up at the last day" (Jn 6:54).

What starts as a simple analogy becomes real. "This is a hard saying; who can listen to it?" say those around you (Jn 6:60). Some people leave; it is too much. Jesus doesn't back down despite their grumblings. He doesn't call them back and say he's speaking symbolically. He lets them go. This is a turning point in his ministry.

At the Last Supper Jesus furthered this teaching in giving us the gift of his Body and Blood in bread and wine. In the consecration at Mass we get the Real Presence of our Savior, body, blood, soul, and divinity. Every Catholic church contains Jesus in the tabernacle. We are able to receive him in Communion, and in Eucharistic adoration, we are able to come to him and just be. We sit in his presence. We gaze at him while he gazes at us.

When we go to him in Eucharistic adoration, we go to him in a special way. We are not approaching a symbol of Jesus; we are approaching the real Jesus. He knows that a symbol isn't enough, so he gave us his real self.

The Real Presence of Jesus in the Blessed Sacrament is a true gift. It is an honor and privilege to pray in front of him. There is peace in his presence. We come as we are, and it is okay. We don't need to worry about how we are dressed or how we look. We don't need to impress him, because he already loves us. He satisfies the hunger within us to be seen. He quenches our thirst for love. When we come to him, bringing our sinfulness and bro-kenness, he pierces our hearts and teaches us to love him more.

To do: Do you truly believe in the Real Presence of Jesus in the Blessed Sacrament? If not, ask Jesus to help you believe — and believe that he will answer your prayer.

To go deeper: Read John 6:25–69. What passage calls to you? Reflect on it.

Spiritual Arsenal

The Lord is my light and my salvation;
*   whom shall I fear?*
The Lord is the stronghold of my life;
*   of whom shall I be afraid?*

Psalm 27:1

An unavoidable consequence of having a deeper relationship with Jesus is spiritual warfare. The devil does not want us to be closer to God. This is nothing to be afraid of, but it is something to be aware of. When you start a practice of adoration, you may notice things getting a little wonky. You may get distracted more easily; your life may get unexpectedly busy; there may be lots of little reasons you can think of to avoid going to adoration; you may experience dryness in prayer; you may feel discouraged in your progress. These are some ways the enemy pokes at us to get us to stop spending time with Jesus.

Here's the good news: Jesus won the war! God is always seeking us, and as God's beloved daughter, you are protected. That doesn't mean spiritual warfare won't happen; it most assuredly will. But you can be prepared. You can recognize it for what it is, and you can be ready. You can keep yourself from falling into despair and discouragement.

Father John Ignatius from the Servants of Christ Jesus in Denver, Colorado, offers seven weapons we can use when we are under attack.*

WEAPON #1: SCRIPTURE

God's word is stronger than the devil. When Jesus was tempted by the devil in the desert, he responded by quoting Scripture. When Satan challenged him to turn the stones to bread, Jesus quoted Deuteronomy 8:3, "It is written, 'Man shall not live by bread alone, but by every word that proceeds from the mouth of God'" (Mt 4:4).

---

* Condensed from a talk by Father John Ignatius, with his permission.

When the devil told him to throw himself off the temple so that the angels could rescue him, Jesus responded with Deuteronomy 6:16: "Again, it is written, 'You shall not tempt the Lord your God'" (Mt 4:7). Finally, when the devil offered all the kingdoms of the world to Jesus if he would bow down and worship him, Jesus answered with Deuteronomy 6:14: "Begone, Satan! For it is written, 'You shall worship the Lord your God and him only shall you serve'" (Mt 4:10).

We can follow his example. Speaking the word of God out loud is powerful. Memorizing long passages of Scripture isn't necessary, but it doesn't hurt to learn a few short ones. Here are a few to get you started:

- Psalm 27:1 The Lord is my light and my salvation; whom shall I fear? The Lord is the stronghold of my life; of whom shall I be afraid?
- Psalm 22:19 But you, O Lord, be not far off! O my help, hasten to my aid!
- Psalm 71:12 O God, be not far from me; O my God, make haste to help me!

WEAPON #2: JESUS' NAME
Just saying the name of Jesus brings him to us and is a prayer.

"Jesus" literally means "God saves." If we call on Jesus, we are not facing the enemy alone.

We can also renew our baptismal promises and pray the Apostles' Creed. (Both can be found in the Common Catholic Prayers chapter in the Catholic Stuff section of this book.)

WEAPON #3: THE LORD'S PRAYER

The "Our Father" is the prayer Jesus taught us (see Mt 6:9–13), and it ends in a request to deliver us from evil. This prayer is a powerful weapon against the devil.

WEAPON #4: PRAISE OF GOD

When the enemy is trying to get our attention, he wants us to get dramatic and despair. We can fight against this by turning our attention to God and praising him. Focus on how awesome God is, and you'll soon find yourself feeling better.

WEAPON #5: INVOKE THE ANGELS

The angels are here to help us. Two angels, in particular, are helpful when we are experiencing spiritual warfare: Saint Michael and Saint Raphael. We also each have a guardian angel whose task is to help us get to heaven. Ask for their help. They will come. (See Common Catholic Prayers for the Saint Michael prayer and the Guardian Angel prayer.)

WEAPON #6: MARY

Mary was elevated by God to be higher than the angels. The devil hates her because as a humble woman, she is higher than he is. Mary is our spiritual mother and will wrap her mantle of love and protection around anyone who asks. By praying the Hail Mary, you are asking her for help, praying Scripture, and invoking Jesus' name. It's an atom bomb of prayer.

WEAPON #7: SACRAMENTALS

Sacramentals are blessed objects such as rosaries, relics, holy water, or medals such as the Miraculous Medal. Sacramentals are used for devotional purposes, and it's important to remember they are not lucky charms or magical items. Sacramentals do not confer the grace of the Holy Spirit in the way that the sacraments do, but by the Church's prayer they prepare us to receive grace and dispose us to cooperate with it (CCC 1670). Sacramentals remind us of the presence of God and the communion of saints. God also allows them to have spiritual properties of protection.

To do: Memorize one of the lines from Scripture under Weapon #1.

To go deeper: Consider which of these weapons you most need, and practice using it regularly.

Part II
Going Deeper

As a relationship unfolds, there is growth. In the beginning of a friendship, whether it develops slowly over time or two people feel an instant connection, there is excitement and anticipation. New friends have much to discuss as they learn about each other, and they want to spend time together. New friends may play their "A game," striving to show only their good side, highlighting those aspects of themselves that they like most and trying to keep the crazy hidden.

Yet there comes a point in any friendship when we have to decide: Is this person someone with whom I feel connected enough to keep going deeper, or are we as close as we'll get?

Some friendships are temporary; others transcend time and place. Consider someone you've known since childhood, or if you're married, your husband. Long-term relationships last because we put effort into maintaining them. We share our real selves even when that real self is a little weepy and vulnerable. We trust the other person with what is important, knowing he or she will guard it with love. We accept help even if our pride screams "no." We walk through life together, sometimes giving and sometimes taking. The more we do this with our friends, the deeper the relationship becomes.

This is just as true in our relationship with Jesus — the original relationship that transcends time and place. It's easy to slip into the mechanics. We show up to Sunday Mass but aren't really present. We skip our daily prayer time because we find so many other things to do. We recite the Our Father or Hail Mary without considering what we are saying. The relationship becomes stagnant because we are just going through the motions.

This section examines what it means to go deeper in our relationship with Jesus. We must be intentional. We have to choose to grow closer to him, and part of that means we need to stop trying to call the shots. We have to accept that he is God and we are not; that we need him, and if we are willing to put down our burdens, he will carry us. We can trust him with our dark side, remembering that he already knows about it and loves us anyway. We surrender and we give him permission to work in us. We humble ourselves to accept his mercy.

We learn this while sitting in adoration with our Lord, and it is here where we can employ our tasks of womanhood, using the gifts God gave us as his beloved daughters. In adoration, we have a chance to pause our lives to worship him, trusting that we will still get it all done. We are attentive to his stirrings in our hearts as we pray, and we try to understand what he is saying. In the presence of Jesus, we grow in communion with him.

Touching His Garment

And Jesus, perceiving in himself that power had gone forth from him, immediately turned about in the crowd, and said, "Who touched my garments?"

Mark 5:30

I love the Gospel story of the hemorrhaging woman. I can picture Jesus on the crowded street, people pushing and trying to be near this remarkable man. He was not surrounded by security guards. He did not keep himself apart. He entered into their midst.

While people yearned, shoved, and inched their way closer, he could feel their touch. Arms against his arms. Shoulders and hips pressing against him. Then he felt power go out of him from one humble, suffering woman who was courageous enough to touch the edge of his cloak. She was convinced that through this tiny point of contact, she would be healed. So she fought her way to him and reached out.

To her surprise, he felt it. She gathered her courage and fell before him, confessing her tremendous act of trust and belief. And he loved her! He called her daughter!

I used to feel I shouldn't ask God for anything, because in comparison to others' needs, my requests were tiny. He has blessed me so abundantly. How could I dare ask for more? How could God possibly have time for me when there are so many others who are suffering?

This Gospel passage gives insight. Despite all the people vying for his attention, Jesus noticed her. She was important to him. She just needed to have faith, to believe that he would hear and answer. It is the same for us. God hears us cry out to him. He values us, and our problems are never too small. He can attend to me while attending to others because he is GOD, the Almighty. Limits of time and space that restrict us do not apply to him.

Once I realized that, I started going to him with everything. He wants us to share our troubles and celebrations with him, because while there are scads of people in the world who need him, he is able to care for every single one of us.

I love imagining Jesus gazing at the woman, a look of kindness and mercy on his face as he reaches down, takes her hand, and gently pulls her to her feet. He says to her lovingly, "Daughter, your faith has saved you. Go in peace."

Those words are not just reserved for that hemorrhaging woman. They are words for us — beloved daughters of God. He desires peace for us. He takes our troubles and sends us off with peace. Even though we are small, he holds our hand and calls us Daughter.

To do: Imagine you are having coffee/tea with Jesus and he asks you about your life. Tell him about your troubles and celebrations.

To go deeper: Read Mark 5:24–34 and imagine you are there. What do you need Jesus to heal in you?

In God's Eyes

Fear not, for I have redeemed you;
I have called you by name, you are mine.

Isaiah 43:1

There's a paradox in the interior life. I struggle to reconcile the reality that I can do nothing, that I am nothing without Jesus. I am selfish and judgmental, quick and shortsighted. My list of flaws is lengthy, and I must approach Jesus as a child. Yet I am a beloved daughter of God. He formed my inner parts. He knitted me in my mother's womb. I am "wonderfully made" (Ps 139 [NABRE]). According to the prophet Isaiah, I was called by name and I am God's. I belong to him. Despite my shortcomings,

I am his. How do I reconcile these things in my head?

What I see in myself each day is a woman who falls. I know the words not said and the uncharitable thoughts. I know when I choose the things of the world over Jesus; when I skip daily Mass or adoration so that I can do something more "fun"; when I continue sharing the gossip while the voice in my head hollers "Stop!" I know these things, and they make me feel unworthy of the love Jesus offers.

Yet God responds, "I have called you by name; you are mine. … You are precious in my eyes, and honored, and I love you" (Is 43:1, 4). God tells me this, and because he is not a God of tricks, nor is he a lying God, I must believe him. This God who made the flower petals with colors that bleed together; this God whose infinite creativity built a world composed of waterfalls and sunrises, mountaintops, crashing seas, and puppies; this God who is wholly responsible for only beauty — this same God made me. I am more than a lucky collision of cells. I am created intentionally by a God who only creates good.

The sin in my life is my fault, but it doesn't change God's vast love for me. Because of his love and desire for me, he calls me to him. I go to adoration to be in his presence. I acknowledge where I fall short, and I rely on the one whose love has no edges. Sitting silently with him, I begin to believe that he made me as his daughter. I truly am his.

I surrender to him all that I am — beautiful and ugly — because he told me I am precious in his eyes. I ask him to help me believe this.

To do: Ask Jesus to give you the grace to believe that you are precious in his eyes, honored, and loved.

To go deeper: Pray with Isaiah 43:1–5. What word or phrase speaks to you? Spend time reflecting on it.

Praising God

*Praise the L*ORD*!*
*Praise the L*ORD *from the heavens,*
praise him in the heights!

Psalm 148:1

I used to feel uncomfortable with the idea of praising God. What possible benefit could God Almighty receive from me telling him he is great? I felt insincere giving praise to God. It was an act of stating the obvious.

My experience with praise in general was limited. When I met my friend Mary, I began to get it. Mary is generous in her praise. She regularly tells me I am awesome. Super simple, not embarrassing or awkward, just a quick, genuine "You're awesome!" slipped into the conversation. I know she means it, too. It isn't hollow or insincere. Mary really believes I am awesome. It makes me feel good to hear those two little words. It makes me feel known and cared about. I wondered why it feels so good, and I realized it's because we don't affirm each other much these days. I'm quick to criticize and find fault, but do I ever state the good? Do I affirm others just because or only when they do something extra? Mary tells me I am awesome for no other reason than I am with her and she appreciates me.

I decided to follow Mary's example and affirm and recognize others. Gradually it has become natural. It feels good to see the good in others. This rosy outlook begins to spill into other parts of life.

Praising God is a good way to start our time in adoration. It focuses our hearts on the bigness of the One we sit before. I realized that for me the secret isn't to give sweeping statements of God's immense glory, but to funnel down to what it is about God that is so great. I looked at details. God created the universe … God created the earth … God created plants … God created flowers … God created dahlias. I love dahlias. Then I give God praise and thanksgiving for the array of dahlias blooming in my backyard. I reflect on their deep colors, how their petals are formed, and how they are a symbol of how he makes beauty from humble beginnings. I praise God for them and for his brilliance in creating them for our enjoyment.

Praising God and others leads to gratitude, and this disposition helps us when the skies in our life are dark and stormy. In the winter, in the polar vortex, when the air is so cold it seems it may snap and nature is asleep, I look at pictures of my dahlias, and I feel grateful and hopeful. God knows us and loves us, and he shows us his love over and over again. We give him thanks through praise, and when it comes from our heart, it feels good and so right.

To do: What small detail of creation are you thankful for? Tell God about it in adoration.

To go deeper: Pray with Psalm 148.

Trust

Trust in the LORD with all your heart,
and do not rely on your own insight.

Proverbs 3:5

I have a great desire to control my life. God gave me free will, after all. If I am able to be self-sufficient, God can spend more time helping those who really need him. Me? I'm doing okay.

That thinking is misguided. True, God did give me free will, and I do need to be active. Sitting back, paralyzed with indecision, won't work. But thinking that I'm okay on my own and that not seeking God's help frees him up to focus on others is not selfless. It's underestimating the power and reach of Jesus. He is

God, and he can do all the things all the time. He is not constrict-ed by human boundaries of time and energy.

My desire to be in full control of my life comes from my lack of trust in God's bigness and his love for me. It is my pride that tells me I can do it on my own. But if I look at my history, I see how wrong I am. The good that has come in my life is from those times when I trusted, when I asked Jesus to be in control, when I sought his will, not mine.

Seeking the will of Jesus requires us to be docile and annoy-ingly patient. Jesus is outside time, and sometimes his perfect plan takes a while to bloom. So we wait; we learn to trust in his goodness and his desire for our welfare. One of the tricks of waiting is to wait actively. If we slog through, worried about how it's going to turn out, anxious because it's taking time, and stuck in indecision, we are not trusting. Trusting Jesus is born of hope. Hope is the certainty that all will be well.

Knowing that Jesus whispers in the silence, we come to him in adoration. We listen. We question. We examine what we are hearing to discern whether it is his will or whether it is our own will trying to trick us. Learning to trust takes time and practice. Our hearts are slower than our heads. We want to trust, and we read in Scripture that we can, but it may not come easily. So we come before our Lord in adoration and ask him to teach us to trust in his tender providence. We offer him our pride and give him permission to work in our lives.

To do: Give Jesus permission to teach you to trust and tell him what the challenge in that will be.

To go deeper: Pray the Litany of Trust found in the Catholic Stuff section of this book.

Like a Child

*The heart of a child does not seek riches and glory
(even the glory of heaven). What this child asks for is
Love. She knows only one thing: to love You, O Jesus.*

Saint Thérèse of Lisieux

When I was a little girl, I was fascinated by Saint Thérèse, the Little Flower. My grade school library had a book about her, and I checked it out several times. Years later, I realized that the Little Flower is a giant of sainthood. She is one of the most frequently quoted saints. Her writings are known around the world.

The lives of many saints are well known in our culture. Saint

Joan of Arc — fought to defend her people and was burned at the stake. Saint Monica — prayer warrior and mother of Saint Augustine. Saint Teresa of Calcutta — selflessly tended to India's poor and sick. Saint Elizabeth Ann Seton — mother and founder of the first free Catholic school in America. I was curious. What made Saint Thérèse of Lisieux a saint? She joined the Carmelites around age fifteen and died at twenty-four. What could a cloistered nun, who died young, possibly have done to become a saint?

It became clear when I read her autobiography, *Story of a Soul*. She did one very simple and very powerful thing, and she did it with her whole being: She loved Jesus. That's it! And it made an ordinary life extraordinary.

She loved Jesus. She dedicated her life to him. She gave every day, every happiness, every struggle to him. He was the center of everything. She fully embraced her place as God's child. She was a model of humility. She wrote, "I am only a child, powerless and weak" (153).

As Jesus wrapped his arms around the children in the Gospel (see Mk 10:16), he wrapped his arms around Saint Thérèse. In her humble, little way, she reveled in her role as God's precious child and taught us to seek this place for ourselves.

We do not have to do great and glorious things, like change

the world or our community. We do not have to be super-stars. We only have to love Jesus as a child loves his parents. In adoration, we approach him with humility, acknowledging how small we really are. We are powerless and weak, and we need Jesus to wrap his arms around us.

When we are in front of the Blessed Sacrament, we embrace our place as his beloved child, and greatness starts. That is when he does extraordinary things through ordinary us. All we have to do is love him and let him in.

To do: Imagine yourself wrapped in the arms of Jesus. Stay there and rest in his love for you. Ask him to teach you how to love him more.

To go deeper: Pray with Saint Thérèse's words quoted above.

Healing

He took our infirmities and bore our diseases.

Matthew 8:17

Each of us is broken. We are surrounded by broken people, and we live in a broken world. We hurt others and ourselves.

Healing is no small thing in the Gospels. Jesus heals many: those who come to him like the leper (see Mt 8:1–4); those who are brought to him (sometimes through dramatic means, such as being lowered through a roof as in Luke 5:17–20); those he encounters in a crowd; those who are brought to his attention by someone else (like the Roman centurion's servant in Luke 7:1–

63

10); and those who don't even ask for healing. Jesus deputizes his apostles to heal as well.

Jesus sees and he heals. Among those who are healed, the common thread is faith. Those who receive Jesus' healing have unwavering belief that Jesus is who he says he is, and that he can and will heal. The hemorrhaging woman believed that if she only touched his cloak, she would be healed — and she was. The centurion, while knowing he was not worthy of Jesus entering under his roof, was certain that with a word, Jesus could and would heal his paralyzed servant. The men who lowered their sick friend through the roof had faith that because of their bold action, their friend would find relief.

In our brokenness, our woundedness, we can come to Jesus in adoration with faith that he will heal us. It may not look like what we expect, but it will be what we need. Sitting in his Real Presence, we bring our wounds. If we come to him in faith, he will be there, the Divine Physician, ready to bind our hurts, fix our broken hearts, and stem the flow of blood from our souls.

In the wideness of his love, God came to us to help us come to him. He made us to need him. He made us incapable of fixing ourselves, and he sent his Son to heal. We need only ask and believe. He is waiting for us in the Blessed Sacrament.

To do: Ask Jesus for healing. Ask him to help you identify where you need his tender care and believe he will help.

To go deeper: Read and pray with Matthew 8:1–17 and 9:1–8.

Hope

It is good that one should wait quietly
for the salvation of the Lord.

Lamentations 3:26

A vacation has three stages: anticipating the trip, preparing for it, and being on it. The first stage is one of hope. It is fun to pore over guidebooks and peruse websites. It is fun looking at the maps of the city and discovering places to explore.

The second stage involves the less enjoyable part — preparing. I am usually eager for the trip itself, but I do not necessarily enjoy the details of arranging dog care and making sure I have all my essentials in 3.4-ounce containers and getting the laundry done so that I have clean clothes and then committing to packing.

It is not unlike our life's journey toward heaven. Reflecting on heaven makes me want to run there immediately. The image of perfect happiness with Jesus is appealing. The idea of being free from the aggravations of earthly life is wonderful. Like a vacation, there is much unknown. What will it be like? What will we do? Whom and what will we see? And as for a vacation, we must prepare.

None of us is worthy of heaven. Our sinful nature gets in the way, and if we dwell on that, heaven can feel like a distant impossibility. Here is where we have the greatest travel agent of all in Jesus. He wants us to get to heaven so much that he humbled himself to come to earth. He suffered, died, and rose from the dead for the forgiveness of our sins so that one day we can be with him. This allows us to excitedly anticipate heaven and know that we can get there.

This is hope. Hope is not wistfully wishing. Hope is desiring eternal happiness with our Lord, who is the object of our hope. It means trusting in Jesus' promises and relying on him, knowing we are dependent on him. (For more on hope, see the *Catechism of the Catholic Church,* 1817). It is through Christ's grace that we are infused with hope.

Hope sustains us as we prepare, as we prune the sinfulness and endure the suffering. It is a gift we dispose ourselves to receive through our time in adoration. When we pause in the scurrying of our life to be with Jesus, he infuses us with hope. Our hope-impregnated souls are sustained when challenges arise. He helps us remember that the things that cause us stress — the laundry, the cooking, the daily giving of ourselves to those around us — are a tiny sliver of our existence, because in heaven we get to enjoy stage three — the being — forever.

While in adoration, we wait quietly with Jesus for our salvation and we listen for his words to help us prepare and remain hopeful.

To do: Ask Jesus to infuse your heart with hope for him, heaven, and eternal happiness.

To go deeper: Pray with Lamentations 3:22–26.

Courage

Be strong and steadfast! Do not fear nor be dismayed,
for the LORD, your God, is with you wherever you go.

Joshua 1:9 (NABRE)

The more we spend time with Jesus, the more we naturally desire to share our experience with others. It's the same as telling one friend how great another friend is and desiring for the two to meet. Jesus is our friend. Our relationship with him is real. Our time spent in adoration, sharing our thoughts and feelings and learning to hear his voice, has cemented this in our hearts. We begin to feel the stirrings of wanting to share this with others. We begin to see the searching in their eyes for something more. We found the source of living water, and we want our thirsty friends to drink.

As women we often desire to create community. We want to include others, be welcoming, be hospitable. And this is good. As Jesus ascended into heaven, he told us to tell others about him, and the apostles spent their remaining years roaming the earth sharing the Good News of salvation.

I wonder what it was like for them. They traveled far to tell people of the Messiah who performed miracles including his own resurrection from the dead. It was an astonishing story, and no doubt they weren't always warmly welcomed. Saint Paul even talks about suffering and being treated shamefully (see 1 Thes 2:2). They needed to be courageous. They knew they were never alone, and it was their joy, honor, and duty to tell others about Jesus.

As you become convicted of God's truth, beauty, goodness, and love, you too may feel these stirrings. Each of us is called in a specific way, whether it is public speaking at conferences, teaching the faith to our children, or simply telling friends about our lived experience with Jesus.

As was Saint Paul, you may be treated shamefully. Sadly, we are in a time when talking about faith is viewed critically and sharing God's truth can yield unpleasant feedback. Like Saint

Paul and the other apostles, though, we can rely on God for the courage we need. We can draw comfort and encouragement from Paul's experience, knowing we are not the first to struggle. We each have a story of how Jesus is part of our life, and no one can take that away. We each know the wonder of sitting with him in adoration. We are learning of his great love for us. We may suffer. We may be scorned or left out. We may even lose friends. It hurts when that happens, but the blessing is that Jesus is the greatest friend we have, and he will make sure that we are okay. As I've started sharing my faith, some people have distanced themselves from me, but the people Jesus has brought into my life have been irreplaceable blessings. He always takes care of us and gives us what we need.

To do: Pray about whom you can share your story with. Ask Jesus to reveal him or her to you.

To go deeper: Pray with Joshua 1:9. Tell Jesus about any fear you may have of telling others about him. Pray for courage.

Part III
Fruits

In this section on fruits of adoration, we will reflect on the gifts Jesus showers on us when we open ourselves to a closer relationship with him. He is so generous. When we spend time in prayer, uniting our heart and will to his, we begin to see changes in ourselves, whether we find we are more patient, more joyful, more peaceful, or more confident in his boundless love for us. The fruits of prayer are real and a wonderful blessing.

Consider a long friendship — a friend you've known since childhood, or your husband. We maintain these relationships out of love for the other but also because we get something from them. Have you ever had a one-sided friendship where you've done all the work? Maybe the only time you get together is when you initiate. Have you ever been the friend of convenience for someone else? She calls when she needs something but isn't there when you need her. Have you had a friendship where it's always about her and rarely about you? We have all experienced this, and these relationships don't last.

A healthy friendship involves both parties giving and taking, growing closer to each other, and benefiting. That may sound selfish, but think about it. A long friendship is a positive growth experience. We become better because of the relationship. We grow to trust, we learn each other's sensitivities and strengths. We learn what to say, how to say it, and when to say it. We emulate what we love in the other person. I have a dear friend whose optimism is inspiring. I love that about her. When I am around her, I find myself growing in enthusiasm for the small things. I have another friend who is deeply connected to the feelings of people on the margins. She is a master at remembering to consider their viewpoint. Being around her has taught me to do the same.

Good fruit comes from good friendships. This is true of our relationship with Jesus as well. In him we have the perfect friend — always available, always listening, and always desiring beauty and wonder for us. As we spend more time with him in adoration, we learn to be like him. In fact, we desire it. As we sit with him and focus our attention on him, he begins to work in our hearts. He helps us see the joy that surrounds us. He helps us be patient in our difficulties and helps us forgive the hurts we carry.

When we come to him and grow more in love with him, he gives us the grace to hear him speaking and to do all that he asks. He offers us protection from the challenges of the world, and his guidance allows us to navigate this journey with peace and to minimize stress and despair. Jesus desires to share abundant good fruit with us. He is calling us to the perfect relationship.

Time

There is need of only one thing. Mary has chosen
the better part and it will not be taken from her.

Luke 10:42 (NABRE)

The story of Martha and Mary in Luke's Gospel presents a clear picture of the battle we all face. I know I should spend time in prayer, and I want to, yet I am pulled toward the many things I think I have to do: my job, caring for my family and home, my own self-care. These things take time — a limited resource. These things are good. It is a blessing to have a satisfying job, a family to serve, and a home to care for. We are not made just for work, but it takes a prominent place in our daily lives.

Where then, does my relationship with God fit in?

I'm kidding myself when I think I can pray first thing in the morning or before bed at night. History has shown that I will fall asleep. Yet once I'm up, fed, and caffeinated, the day has already taken off, and finding space to squeeze in some time with Jesus is a challenge. What Jesus told his disciples is real for me as well: my spirit is willing, but my flesh is weak.

This experience is mirrored in the story of Mary and Martha. Jesus comes to their home, and Martha launches into service mode. Jesus is an honored guest; it is fitting that he be given food and drink. Mary chooses differently. She sits at his feet and listens to what he is teaching. I imagine how I would respond if Jesus walked into my house unexpectedly. I would rush around picking up backpacks, errant shoes, and tufts of dog hair. I'd get to work tidying up and searching for food to prepare. This desire to show hospitality and care for others is written on us, and it is good.

But Jesus reminds us of what is better. He gently tells Martha that Mary has made the better choice in sitting with him. This is a powerful message. The work we do is good, but being with Jesus is better. He is giving us permission to pause the carnival ride of our life and sit with him.

Taking time to go to adoration may feel like an unrealistic

sacrifice. Instead, try to see it as an act of love and trust. In attending adoration, we are telling Jesus that he is more important than our work. We love him above the work. We are also telling him we trust that making him our priority is most important. We are spending our limited resource of time with the One who loves us and wants us to be with him.

In the end, what needs to get done will get done. The rest will wait for tomorrow, and nothing bad will happen. God has a way of stretching time, and when we put him first, he helps us. We are able to get our tasks done, often better and more cheerfully.

To do: Ask Jesus to help you trust that, by investing time with him, all will get done.

To go deeper: Pray with the story of Mary and Martha in Lukw 10:38–42. Are you Mary sitting at Jesus' feet, or Martha scurrying around preparing? What does Jesus say to you?

God's Abundant Love

Surely goodness and mercy shall follow
me all the days of my life;
and I shall dwell in the house of the LORD for ever.

Psalm 23:6

One of the fruits of adoration is great love for Jesus, and as we grow more in love with him, he reveals how great his love is for us. It's a love that is wide and deep, a love we are unable to fully grasp. His love is so extravagant that he came to earth to live among us. While fully divine, he was also fully human, and he suffered a painful death, taking on our sin so that we may live with him forever in heaven.

Why do God's love and generosity stir feelings of amazement and surprise? The Bible is clear. The story of salvation history is not full of code that we need to puzzle through to understand. In fact, one of the first things the Holy Spirit did at Pentecost was give the apostles the ability to communicate in different languages so that everyone who heard them would understand. The message of God's unsurpassed love for us is simple, yet every time I encounter that love, I am amazed. Then I wonder why it amazes me. My head knows its truth, my heart experiences its glory, but still it leaves me astounded every single time.

Perhaps this love is so amazing because we don't get it anywhere else. We try to love as Jesus does, but we cannot. Yet despite our failings, he loves us and forgives us. When we stumble, he picks us up. He gives us graces we don't deserve, and then he gives us more. He buries us under an avalanche of his love for no reason other than that he created us as his beloved daughters. We didn't earn it.

How do we respond to this dramatic love? Two ways: We gratefully and humbly receive it, recognizing it as pure gift; and then we glorify God who is love.

We know our sins, we question if we are worthy, we wonder how we can accept such extravagance, and we may want to hide in shame. But God's love is freely given, and it is good to accept.

We may not be worthy in our own eyes or the eyes of the world, but in the eyes of the Creator we are worthy and worth it. We praise God, Father, Son, and Holy Spirit, though he has no need of praise. We offer it because it is what we have, and it is beautiful to him.

To do: Write a love letter to Jesus telling him about your love for him.

To go deeper: Pray with Psalm 23.

Joy

May the God of hope fill you with all joy and
peace in believing, so that you may abound
in hope by the power of the holy Spirit.

Romans 15:13

When my daughter was very young, we had plans to do something a child of her age would enjoy, and we had to cancel them. Her brothers were, understandably, disappointed, but her response was "OK!" and she bounced off to play. Each new day was filled with possibility for the lass. She launched into everything she did with enthusiasm, whether playing with her dollhouse, playing with a friend, or reading a book. Life was joyful, and it radiated from her.

During the COVID-19 lockdown in the spring of 2020, my daughter was not happy to have her freshman year of college interrupted. She was not happy to be away from her wonderful new friends and stuck at home with her parents and brothers. Despite the tears and frustration, though, she was still joyful. Her daily practice of adoration and Mass had prepared her for this challenge.

Her internal joy is enviable and is a gift the Holy Spirit gave her at a young age. It's not to be confused with happiness, which is of this world and influenced by external events. Happiness is fleeting. Joy is otherworldly, and its source is internal. We can have a joyful disposition even when life is hard and we are unhappy.

Most of us are not born with the gift of joy already written on our hearts, but that doesn't mean it is out of reach. Just like for my daughter, a regular, intentional prayer life helps us develop this beautiful fruit. When we spend time in the Real Presence of Jesus, we experience his gracious love. It swells our hearts and permeates our souls. We feel gratitude for this love, and this gratitude leads to joy because we learn that while we feel like we can't control our little section of the world, all will be okay. We learn to let go of the things that don't matter (where we live, the car we drive, how popular we are, or if the house is clean enough for our mother-in-law to visit), and focus on that which does matter: our place as beloved daughters of God, our inherent beauty and value, and the hope of eternal life with Jesus.

Joy is a gift given to us because of God's great love, and our time in adoration prepares our hearts to accept it.

To do: Compose a prayer to Jesus asking him for the gift of joy.

To go deeper: Share with Jesus the things that are robbing you of joy and ask for his guidance in letting go of them.

Patience

*For I know the plans I have for you, says
the Lord, plans for welfare and not for evil,
to give you a future and a hope.*

Jeremiah 29:11

A while back, I was in a season of discernment, and after seven months of waiting for God's answer, I had grown frustrated. I knew — in my head — that God has his own timeline, and it is the perfect timeline. But my heart was impatient. I now refer to that time as the Great Wait, because in the end it took a year. And while I tried to be patient and trust, I fell down many, many times in anger and frustration.

Patience and endurance are closely linked. Both have an element of adversity. *Merriam Webster's* (11th edition) defines being patient as "bearing pains or trials calmly or without complaint, being steadfast." Endurance is withstanding hardship. Most people do not come by these virtues naturally. They must be developed, and the only way is by going through a difficult time. A rosy life does not create a patient person; however, a patient person can create a rosy life.

Saint Paul exhorts the Hebrews, "For you have need of endurance, so that you may do the will of God and receive what is promised" (Heb 10:36). He continues, "We are not of those who shrink back and are destroyed, but of those who have faith and keep their souls" (Heb 10:39).

We read of Abraham patiently waiting for promised descendants; of both Sarah and Elizabeth finally bearing a child in their old age; and Simeon who was promised by the Lord that he would not die until he saw Christ. They waited. They endured.

They did not do it alone, though. They had God's help, and so do we. There will be times of adversity in our lives that we cannot avoid. There will be times when we may wonder why it is taking so long to see the good. These are the times when our practice of adoration reveals its fruit. When we encounter these challenges, we will find ourselves able to endure. We will find pockets of patience we did not know we had because they are graces from God.

When we invest in our relationship with Jesus, when we give him what is precious to us, he takes care of us. It is not because we earned it or deserve it. We certainly are not worthy. It is because he loves us.

To do: Where in your life do you need patience? Tell Jesus about it.

To go deeper: Pray with Jeremiah 29:11.

Faithfulness

God is faithful, and by him you were called to
fellowship with his Son, Jesus Christ our Lord.

1 Corinthians 1:9 (NABRE)

The Israelites were a lamenting people. Desert life was hard, for the desert offers little to sustain. They wished they had never left Egypt, desiring slavery over freedom. While enslaved, they had food and shelter. In the desert, they were without. They grumbled. They did not yet see what good was ahead of them. They did not yet trust in God's abundance. They were hungry and uncomfortable, and they complained.

How often are we like the Israelites? We grouse. We dwell on the bad. We lament. We do not yet see the Lord's blessings amidst the quotidian routine. We spiral into a hole of discouragement, and the shining light above us seems so far away.

It is in these times of desert that we can turn to our God and cry out as the Israelites did. God did not ignore them. Instead, he rained bread from the sky and sent quail. Each day they had what they needed, and that is key. It may not have been what they wanted or thought they wanted, but it was what they needed, and it was lovingly lavished on them by a patient and understanding Father.

God desires to shower blessings on us as well. He wants us to be happy. He created us for communion with him. His plan is perfect. Being human, we forget these things. We assume that because he didn't give us what we want, he doesn't love us. But he gives us what we need, and our faith in his goodness helps us recognize that blessing.

We can have faith that God loves us without boundaries. Jesus died on the cross so that we can be united to him and the Father eternally in heaven. Jesus "suffered, died, and was buried and on the third day he rose." All for us, each and every one of us, now, then, and to come. This was the mission of the One who loves us. Our Lord is not deceitful. He does not trick us or play mind games. He invites us to be with him and asks us for our trust.

The more time we spend in front of the Blessed Sacrament, the easier it is to be faithful. We deepen our relationship with Jesus. We learn to hear him and notice his movement in our lives. We surrender to his will, and we live in his love. We are faithful.

To do: Recommit yourself to spending time in adoration with Jesus and tell Jesus why you desire to make this commitment.

To go deeper: Ask Jesus to give you boundless faith and extravagant hope in him. Ask him to help you surrender to his will.

Protection

But the Lord is faithful; he will strengthen
you and guard you from the evil one.

2 Thessalonians 3:3 (NABRE)

Written on our female souls is the desire to be pursued and protected. It feels good when a man holds a door open or offers to carry a heavy package. It doesn't subtract from our own inherent strength, because chivalry is born of respect. It is also not an either/or supposition; instead it is both/and. We are both fierce like Saint Joan of Arc and gentle like the Blessed Virgin Mary. We are capable, and we desire protection.

Jesus pursues and protects us in a way that brings comfort

to our soul. It is a beautiful love story that speaks to our desire to be found, and Jesus desires to find us. When we go to him in adoration, we are meeting the one who finds us irresistible, and we spend time under his protective gaze.

We are like sheep. We are soft with a strong herd instinct. We long for a shepherd because we are vulnerable to the evil wolf who hurts us. We get caught up following the herd, but much of the herd has abandoned our Good Shepherd and struck out on its own. The wolf rejoices. We have forgotten how much we need our shepherd to guide and protect us from evil. The wolf has convinced our herd that our shepherd doesn't exist anymore. The pasture is safe. We do not need our shepherd; we only need ourselves and our herd.

But the wolf is here. He has infiltrated and convinced us of his lies: lies about our value and lovableness, lies about our capabilities and worthiness. We are not safe. We need our shepherd.

When we wander away, our shepherd Jesus calls us. Like sheep, we learn to recognize the voice of our shepherd in our quiet prayer. We learn to follow the shepherd we know. The wolf is wily, but he is not our shepherd. Jesus is the voice we must follow, even it if means not following the herd. Jesus will never lead us astray. His desire is to love us. We learn to listen to his loving words, and we rejoice in our need for him and his protecting presence.

Listen for our shepherd's voice, not the wolf's. He will take care of you and protect you from evil, and you will never die. He has already won. We just need to listen. As we spend time in adoration, we grow closer to our shepherd and more confident of his protection.

To do: What lies is the wolf telling you? Bring them to Jesus.

To go deeper: Pray with John 10:7–18; imagine yourself as the sheep and Jesus as your Shepherd. What is he saying to you in the passage?

Grace

*But grace was given to each of us according
to the measure of Christ's gift.*

Ephesians 4:7

Joseph, Jesus' foster father, was a dreamer. God spoke to him as he slept, first telling him Jesus had been conceived by the Holy Spirit, then warning him of impending danger from Herod and instructing him to take his holy family to Egypt. Then at the right time, God spoke to him in a dream again, sending them back to Israel. I think about Joseph and these dreams. How did he know they weren't crazy nighttime ideas hatched by a tired brain? Yet Joseph trusted that what he was dreaming was God speaking, and he obeyed. Maybe "dream" is a metaphor to help us understand. Maybe the dreams were unusually vivid. It doesn't matter. Joseph heard and obeyed.

How did he know? The answer is: God's grace. God had a plan. God knew Joseph was a good man who loved God and desired to serve him. God gave him what he needed — the grace, the confidence, the conviction — so that he would hear and obey. We don't read that Joseph woke up, shook his head, and muttered to himself that last night's dinner could have been cooked more. No, we read that Joseph acted. His faithfulness kept God's plan for salvation moving forward.

God speaks to us as well, and sometimes what we hear is unexpected or challenging. Perhaps he nudges us to speak to a certain person. Perhaps he pushes us to put down our phone and read. Perhaps he inspires us to go somewhere new for our morning coffee. We don't know why, but we obey. We obey because we love God, and he gives us the grace to do so.

Regular people do amazing things for God. People like us touch others in beautiful ways, live the Gospel, and make the world better because God inspires this in us. It has nothing to do with being more special or more holy. It is grace. With grace, humble, broken people assist in building the kingdom of God.

We can and should ask for graces we need, and particularly

for graces we need that we don't even know we need. When we sit in front of Jesus in adoration, he gazes on us and we on him, and our hearts can cry out for what we need to love him and live as his daughters. His grace is powerful. It is mighty. It makes the difference.

To do: Quiet your heart and ask for the grace you need for today. Don't worry about tomorrow. Think of what you need today as God's beloved daughter.

To go deeper: Pray with Matthew 1 (feel free to skip the genealogy list). Pray for the grace to fully trust in God's wishes and to desire to be his instrument.

Part IV
Stumbling Blocks

As a relationship deepens and matures, problems inevitably appear. Sometimes it is the busyness of life that keeps us from prioritizing the relationship. When our children were little, I remember struggling to find time to invest in friendships with people who weren't in the same stage of life I was. Sometimes, it is a difference in opinion that creates trouble in a friendship. It takes respect and patience to deeply listen to someone with whom we disagree. Sometimes it's a hurtful word or action that causes a rift. We need humility to admit we were wrong, and bravery to tell someone else when we are hurt.

We also bring to our friendships our brokenness and idio-syncrasies. The wounds we carry from past relationships have an inconvenient way of getting mixed up in current ones. If our trust has been violated, it is hard to trust again. If we were be-trayed, we may worry it will happen again. The reality is that we can be a hot mess at times, and we cannot — and should not — hide that from the people who love us.

The same is true in our relationship with Jesus. Prayer can get dry, and while that's a natural part of the interior life, it makes us wonder if something is wrong. Sometimes we get wrapped up in worrying and forget to rest in God. Sometimes we are lonely and feel far from Jesus, unknown and unseen. We desire con-trol in our lives, and surrendering ourselves in adoration means giving up that control. We also feel unworthy of going to Jesus. We know we are frail and sinful. We know where we've messed up, and we know that Jesus knows it too. Finally, sometimes we have trouble slowing ourselves down and being quiet. We are action-oriented and results-driven people. Adoration is a time of stillness and waiting.

Whatever it is, whether one of these scenarios or something unique to you, there are, for all of us, things that get in the way of a regular practice of adoration. The good news is that, as in any relationship, the hard times, when weathered together, draw us closer to the one we love. The hard times are when we face our sinfulness head-on and are reminded again of God's overwhelming love for us. When we push through the dry times, when we throw our sorry selves at the foot of the Cross, when we are honest about our feelings, Jesus doesn't leave. Others may, but Jesus never does.

Dryness in Prayer

Fear not, for I am with you.

Isaiah 43:5

Sometimes when I pray, I don't know what to say. Sometimes I don't want to say anything. Sometimes I feel like I showed up, but Jesus didn't. Sometimes I don't want to be there at all.

The truth is, sometimes prayer gets hard. We call these times periods of dryness. We feel frustrated and alone. We remember times when it felt good and easy to pray and wonder why it got so hard. We worry that Jesus has lost interest and doesn't hear us. It can be scary.

When these times come (and they happen to everyone), we

find comfort in God's word. In Isaiah 43, we read:

> I have called you by name, you are mine.
> When you pass through the waters I will be with you;
> and through the rivers, they shall not overwhelm you;
> when you walk through fire you shall not be burned,
> and the flame shall not consume you.
> Because you are precious in my eyes,
> and honored, and I love you.
> Fear not, for I am with you. (Isaiah 43:1b–2, 4–5)

There it is, right in the Bible: God reminding us we are never alone. He is with us in times of difficulty. We need not fear.

Faith resides in our head and our heart. We know it in our head, and sometimes we feel it in our heart. Feelings are not an indication of God's presence, though. There may be times we don't feel it, and we have to remember what God told us through Isaiah. We remember, in our head, that he is still there. He promised he will not leave us, and God does not break his promises. When prayer feels hard, dry, and useless, we cling to that knowledge.

In times of dryness, we need fidelity and perseverance. Even when we don't feel like praying, we must keep at it. In his book *Time for God*, Father Jacques Philippe writes: "What matters is not whether our mental prayer is beautiful, or whether it works, or whether it is enriched by deep thoughts and feelings, but whether it is persevering and faithful. It is faithfulness alone that enables the life of prayer to bear wonderful fruit. Mental prayer is basically no more than an exercise in loving God. But there is no true love without fidelity."

Prayer is loving God, and being faithful in prayer is fruitful, even if you aren't feeling the feelings you think you should be feeling. There will be times when you have to drag yourself to adoration and times when you are distracted or frustrated while there. You may not know how or what to pray. At these times, you must persevere. In the back of this book are many beautiful Catholic prayers you can turn to when your own words won't come to you. Pick one out and pray it slowly, meditating on each line.

To do: Express your sadness, frustration, or confusion to Jesus in your prayer. Ask him to teach you to deal with dry periods.

To go deeper: Pray with Isaiah 43:1–5. Ask the Holy Spirit what he wants you to attend to in this passage and spend some time with it.

Anger

*I have heard your prayer; I have seen
your tears. Now I am healing you.*

2 Kings 20:5 (NABRE)

Anger is a natural human emotion. If you've ever been angry at God, you're not the first, and you're not alone. There are times it feels as though God has forgotten about me or is ignoring me. There are times I don't like the situation I find myself in — it wasn't what I planned, it is disappointing, and it doesn't feel like the good he promised in Jeremiah 29:11. Sometimes I get angry at injustice in the world or at the sadness or suffering of someone I love. Sometimes I am angry at my own suffering.

God feels far away in these times.

Several of the psalms express the anger and bafflement we often feel toward God. Take just a few examples:

> How long, LORD? Will you utterly forget me?
> How long will you hide your face from me?
> How long must I carry sorrow in my soul,
> grief in my heart day after day? (Psalm 13:2–3 [NABRE])

> Why, LORD, do you stand afar
> and pay no heed in times of trouble? (Psalm 10:1 [NABRE])

> My God, my God, why have you abandoned me? (Psalm 22:2 [NABRE])

We sense the agony, the feeling of being abandoned and alone, wondering where God is and when he will come back. It is comforting to know that I am not the first to feel this way, but it does not take my anger away. I feel guilty that I am mad at the one who has blessed me with so much. I feel ashamed for my selfishness. I try to push the feeling away, and I stop praying because I feel hypocritical. How can I dare approach Jesus when I am mad at him?

I confessed this anger once, and the priest assured me that it is okay to be mad at Jesus. He can take it. He encouraged me to tell Jesus how I felt. Raging *at* Jesus is not a great idea, but expressing my anger *to* him is important. That night in adoration I told him how mad I was. I told him how worried I was. I told him I was not happy with the situation and I wanted it to be over. Relief flooded me as this burden I had been carrying was released, and nothing horrible had come of me being mad at God. Instead, Jesus comforted me and reminded me that I am loved.

As you grow in your practice of adoration, you will become more confident that you can bring these feelings to Jesus and not be rebuked. You can sit in front of him and share your anger, disappointment, and frustration. He will take it and give you his comfort. In the safety of his presence, you will find peace.

To do: Have you ever been mad at God? Tell him about it.

To go deeper: Pray with the verse from 2 Kings above and allow God to speak these words to you in your pain.

Fear

And he awoke and rebuked the wind, and
said to the sea, "Peace! Be still!"

Mark 4:39

I was afraid while writing this. Writing a book is a longtime
dream, and I was beset with doubt and fear. Will my editor dis-
cover I'm a fraud? Will I lose all the words I love so dearly? Will I
be laughed at? Will anyone read it? For months after signing the
contract, I had writer's block. It was my own stormy boat. I knew
Jesus had not abandoned me, but I couldn't seem to wake him up
and get his attention. I was afraid I was going to fail.

The months wore on, and the words came back. It wasn't

smooth or easy, but I began to make forward progress. Each week I took my notebook to adoration and asked Jesus to give me the words he wanted me to write. He was there, as he always is. There were times when I lost the words and times I was convinced I had no business writing a book, but Jesus was awake in the stern of this tossed-around boat of a manuscript. He calmed the wind and my heart. He helped me be still and keep facing forward.

Each of us has fears, whether it is a fear that we will fail, a fear that we will lose our loved one and be left alone, or a fear of being unseen and unloved. We may fear the unknown, a loss of control, or sickness. We may fear hunger, joblessness, or for our safety. What we learn in our time spent in adoration of Jesus Christ is that we are not alone. Jesus is in the Host in the monstrance, and his presence there is just as real as when he was in the boat with the disciples. And just as when he commanded the wind and the waves to be still, he brings us that same peace.

The disciples were brave enough to ask him for help. We can do the same. Jesus is in front of us waiting for us to ask for help with our fear. And we can have faith that even if he seems to be asleep, he is not. He is listening and caring. He will let us know in his special, quiet way that he is present.

To do: What are you afraid of? Share it with Jesus and ask him for help.

To go deeper: Pray with Mark 4:35–41, imagining you are in the boat on that stormy night while Jesus sleeps. What do you feel? What will you do or not do?

Worry

Pray, hope, and don't worry. Worry is useless.
God is merciful and will hear your prayer. Have
courage and do not fear the assaults of the devil.

Padre Pio

While worry is a useless emotion, it's also a common one. Our worry ranges from small concerns such as accomplishing all the tasks on our to-do list, to larger ones such as the safety of a loved one, to silly ones such as what others will think. There is no good outcome to worry. It does not spur us forward; rather it glues us in place, helpless and afraid.

I have a friend with cancer, and we do not know the prognosis. It is hard not to worry. My prayer is that of desperation, begging God for what I want. Then I go back to worrying, which will have no good outcome. It will not change his diagnosis. It will mostly serve to keep me feeling helpless and afraid, and I cannot be a supportive friend when I am a wreck.

My concern for him and his family compels me to pray for healing. My faith in Jesus tells me to pray that God's will be done. How do I marry the two? One more thing to worry about — how to pray.

In these times of worry, whether for a big thing or a small thing, it is good to go to Jesus in adoration. Jesus will remind us that we are deeply loved by our Creator, and we can believe that he is taking care of us. He wants to give us freedom to enjoy life and peace that all will be well. Worry is not part of his plan for us.

But how do we stop the worry? How do we release it? How do we control it instead of letting it control us? This is where a regular practice of adoration is helpful. When we sit in front of our Savior, we can give the worry to him. Instead of allowing it to keep us from God, we bring it to him. We can be assured of his support when we ask him to help us let it go. The antidote to worry is trust in God and surrendering control to him.

When we release the worry, we open ourselves to a refreshing life of freedom and peace with the knowledge that God, who loves us more than we know, will take care of us, come good or bad.

To do: What are you worrying about needlessly? Ask Jesus for help letting go of it and trust that he will take care of it.

To go deeper: Pray with Matthew 6:25–26. What is Jesus saying to you personally?

Loneliness

And when they had eaten their fill, he told
his disciples, "Gather up the fragments
left over, that nothing may be lost."

John 6:12

If Jesus is concerned about scraps of bread, how much more must he be concerned for us?

We all desire to be seen and heard. We long to be noticed. In a world where many people are focused on themselves, we feel lonely. We seek others' validation. We curate our image on social media. We put up notices challenging others to repost it as proof that they see us. It's easy to feel alone and unnoticed when no one puts a heart or thumbs-up on something we share. We value our virtual friends and long for their attention. We wonder if we are forgotten.

What we know from the Bible is that we are not forgotten. Jesus cares about the fragments; we can be confident that the Lord will never forget us (see Is 49:15). We are held in his palm. Jesus is more than a virtual friend. He is a true friend who is always pursuing us. He comes to us in our messiness, and heaven rejoices when we turn toward him.

It's easy to assume that if others forget us, Jesus will too. This feeling of aloneness is not from God; it's from the enemy. The devil is trying to keep us from our rightful place with Jesus. When we feel lonely, it is even more important to go to Jesus in adoration. Jesus patiently waits for us in the Eucharist. When we go to him in adoration, he is always there and always available. He calls us to his heart.

Not only do we have a perfect friend in Jesus, we have a holy trove, a cheering section of angels and saints led by none other than the first and perfect disciple, the Blessed Virgin Mary. Each of us has a guardian angel assigned at our birth, an angel whose mission is to help us get to heaven. We have the saints — holy men and women who walked before us — in heaven now, ready to pray for us.

And we have the consolation of the holiest saint of all, Mary, who at the foot of the cross agreed to be our spiritual mother, and who never ceases pointing us to her Son. When we call out to her, she wraps us in her mantle of love. With the host of angels and saints, we are assured that we are never alone. God has sent us his Son and given us the Holy Spirit, but in his generosity, God our Father wants to give us even more. When we feel like a leftover fragment, we can be certain that we are not forgotten. There are many in heaven praying for us.

To do: Spend some time considering the angels and saints in heaven interceding just for you.

To go deeper: With confidence that you will be heard, pray for intercession from your own guardian angel, a favorite saint, and/or Mary.

Feeling Unworthy

The LORD is merciful and gracious,
slow to anger and abounding in mercy.

Psalm 103:8

At the peak of a hot desert day, a lone woman approaches a well to draw water. She dares not come in the cooler morning because she is a sinful woman, and she is not welcome when the others are there. She meets Jesus at that well. Instead of shunning her as many would, he talks with her. He knows about her sinful life and still speaks gently and lovingly to her.

I imagine the sun and heat. I imagine her thirst. It is more than a physical need for water; it is a spiritual need for living water, and Jesus offers it to her. She is honest with him about her sins, and he doesn't condemn her. He reveals himself to her. She leaves to tell others about him.

Jesus meets us also. We may be afraid to go to him in adoration. We may be acutely conscious of our sinfulness and feel unworthy. We may feel rejected by others and assume that Jesus will reject us as well. We may wonder how he could want us to come to him when we fall short so often.

It is in this uncertainty that he arrives. He summons us to himself and offers us mercy. We can tell him what's on our hearts and where we struggle. We can be honest about our sins, as was the woman at the well, and likewise Jesus will offer us living water. His mercy is not reserved for a few special people. It is for all of us.

When we sit in front of him in adoration, we consider that mercy. We accept it as an undeserved but beautiful gift. When I pray with my own unworthiness, it leads me to a deep feeling of gratitude because despite my hang-ups, Jesus still calls me to himself. In Psalm 103, we are reminded of God's goodness. He does not anger quickly; instead he forgives quickly. "He does not deal with us according to our sins, nor repay us according to our iniquities. For as the heavens are high above the earth, so great is his mercy toward those who fear him" (Ps 103:10–11).

Jesus is always calling us, inviting us deeper toward his heart. He knows us, and still he calls. We can dare sit in front of him in adoration because he forgives our sins. We can be assured of this. As we build a habit of adoration, we become more comfortable with his mercy, and it creates within us a disposition of thankfulness.

To do: Write a short prayer to Jesus asking him to help you accept his mercy.

To go deeper: Pray with Psalm 103.

Judgment

Neither do I condemn you; go and do not sin again.

John 8:11

Imagine the woman caught in adultery, and I wonder about her. What led her to this serious sin? It is easy to take on the role of judge and assume she is just an immoral woman, a woman who deserves what she gets. It's easy to feel superior to her and condemn her bad decision. The law demands she be stoned. Surely she knew when she engaged in adultery the risk of death by stoning. She did it anyway. It's easy to feel this way toward her.

Imagining this scene again, instead of a defiant, hardened

woman, I see a fragile, scared one. She is hastily dressed, her hair is disheveled, and she is rightly terrified because she knows she is facing a painful death. I wonder what brought her to such a place. Was her adultery an act of desperation? Was she exchanging her body for food for her hungry children? Maybe she confused it with love. Having never been truly loved and respected, perhaps she thought this was what love is. Or maybe, she hated herself and engaged in unhealthy acts to dull the pain of her misery.

When I consider these scenarios, I feel less judgment and more compassion. Mine has not been the perfect Catholic life. There have been missteps along the way and some things I'll probably wrestle with until the end of my time. All of us can look back at misguided or ill-advised decisions with regret and remorse. Some were born of desperation, some of arrogance, some of ignorance, and some of stupidity. Some we continue to carry with us, and they prevent us from growing in relationship with Jesus. *How could he ever forgive/love/want me, given what I've done?* we wonder.

The challenge lies in recognizing that Jesus wants to meet us in these very things, if we let him. Instead of wishing to stone us, Jesus forgives us. When we bring our sinful past to him in adoration, we allow him to help us forgive ourselves. But he gives us important words, the same words he spoke to the woman caught in adultery: "Go and do not sin again." He doesn't condemn us when we are honest about our shortcomings, and he challenges us to refrain from that sin again.

Don't let a sinful past keep you from adoration. He is waiting for you. Don't assume you aren't good enough. He is calling you. Go to him and be loved.

To do: What past sin(s) do you need to bring to Jesus in adoration? Tell him about it, and promise to do better with the help of his grace.

To go deeper: Pray with John 8:2–11. Imagine you are the woman caught in adultery and Jesus is talking to you. What does he say?

Noise

My soul, be at rest in God alone,
from whom comes my hope.

Psalm 62:6 (NABRE)

In 1989, Depeche Mode released a music video showing a man carrying a chair through various landscapes — up a mountain, across cliffs, and through snow. In each new location, he sat down and looked out across the scenery. The video concludes with him in his chair, and we hear "Enjoy the silence."

Imagine what it must be like, alone in nature, away from the sounds of the world, hearing only the sounds God gave us — the wind, the birds, and his still, small voice. How many of us fear the silence? What happens when the din of the world goes away? What is left?

When we go to Eucharistic adoration, we are in silence. The church or chapel is a silent space. Sometimes, this can be daunting. What will I hear when it is just me and Jesus? When I pull off the distractions and just breathe, will I be okay with what is left? When I am not filling time but letting it wash over me, what will there be?

What I have found is that when I stop and am quiet, I begin to know the one who loves me is near. He is summoning me closer to him. My pulse slows, my hands open, my shoulders relax. My body feels heavy.

This does not come easily or naturally. My brain prefers spinning. It takes time — sometimes just a few minutes, sometimes many minutes — to quiet everything down. I have to recognize the importance of this time with Jesus and trust that in investing it with him, I will still accomplish all I need to. So I try to leap off the hamster wheel and enter into the peace of Jesus' presence, where I can hear his whisper. I try to set aside my worries and my to-do list. I learn to trust in his goodness, in his desire for my welfare.

To do: Make a quick list of the things that are distracting you and offer them to Jesus. Tell him of your desire to be silent with him. If your mind wanders, gently bring it back. Have patience as you learn to be quiet.

To go deeper: Pray with Psalm 62, focusing on the words of the psalmist and how they speak to you.

Control

*Do not fear: I am with you; do not be anxious: I am
your God. I will strengthen you, I will help you, I
will uphold you with my victorious right hand.*

Isaiah 41:10 (NABRE)

A few years ago, I experienced a time in my life of being in-be-
tween. One season ended and the next had not yet been revealed. The message I received in prayer was WAIT; and while I
pushed back on that idea, God was clear that I was in a season of
waiting. I am one who likes to plan, and this experience became
a yearlong lesson of learning to let go of my desire to control my
future and instead wait for the Lord.

I have had several friends describe themselves as having "control issues." It brings me an odd sense of comfort to know I am not alone in this, but it doesn't help me let go of this desire to call the shots in my life. For years as a stay-at-home mother, I controlled the flow of the days. I set the daily schedule and managed our activities. When I was cast into a time of uncertainty, it was a challenge I was struggling to rise to. I wanted to seek out the next adventure and start working toward it. I wanted action. I wanted purpose to the empty day yawning ahead of me each morning. God disagreed.

It is hard to pray when God isn't handling a situation the way we want. What got me through was Eucharistic adoration. In his message to wait was an invitation to wait with him. Jesus invited me to bring the worry about the future and the frustration of not being in control to him. I imagined I had a burlap sack stuffed with these unsavory feelings that I dragged down the church aisle and dumped in front of the monstrance. I told him I was mad, I told him I was worried, and I begged him for help. He accepted that bag of awfulness and over time taught me patience and trust in his plan.

In the sometimes-ungraceful waiting, I learned I can trust God and that he will indeed strengthen me. And while I didn't know it when I was in the middle, it was a time of life I would not trade. Going to Jesus in adoration helped me even when I couldn't tell it was helping. God worked in my heart in many ways that later revealed themselves. Being with Jesus brought me comfort in a time of confusion. A year later, when the season finally came to an end, I felt closer to Jesus, and if I had not had that time waiting with him, I would not be who I am today.

God knows us better than we know ourselves, and he knows that we want to drive the bus of our life. When we allow him to be in control, though, we open ourselves to loving him more deeply and we experience the good he desires for us. We can be confident in Isaiah's words that God is helping us and holding us. These words are true.

To do: Give Jesus your own sack of unsavory feelings and ask him to help you. Be specific in what you need.

To go deeper: Pray with Isaiah 41:10 and listen for God's voice.

Part V
Catholic Stuff

One of the great blessings of the Catholic Faith is its richness. In it we find two thousand years of tradition and a treasure trove of prayer and wisdom. There is great comfort in knowing we are part of something beautiful and ancient.

God loves our simple words born of our hearts much as a mother loves the artwork of her children. Her children may not be as talented as Caravaggio, but a mother accepts her children's work with delight. In the same way, we may not be as eloquent in prayer as Saint Thomas Aquinas, but God lovingly accepts and cherishes our prayer.

But there are times when we have no words, or the words we have do not adequately express what is in our hearts. That's what this final section is for. I hope you will find here a Catholic toolbox to rescue you when prayer just won't seem to come. In this section, you will find prayers both old and new that express joy, pain, and a host of emotions in between. Some are written by saints, some by religious, some are from the Bible, and some are from ordinary people. Each one in its unique way helps us communicate with our heavenly Father and his Son. Each helps express something inexpressible.

Feel free to turn to this section when you need to. I pray you'll find here prayers that provide you a way to enjoy even deeper communication with God.

The Rosary

The origin of the Rosary is unclear. There is a tradition linking the origins of the Rosary to Saint Dominic, but that is not substantiated. We know that Mary told the Fatima visionaries to pray the Rosary daily.

Saint Faustina, who recounts many conversations with Jesus in her diary, also encourages people to pray the Rosary. In addition, Saint John Paul II, Saint Teresa of Calcutta, Padre Pio, Saint Louise de Marillac, Saint Louis de Monfort, and Saint Francis de Sales were great champions of the Rosary.

The Rosary is one of my favorite prayers. It is simple and powerful. I have found it to be one of the best ways to quiet myself and hear God speak. I think of my mind as having two parts: The front part is where the action is — the worrying, planning consciousness of what is happening around me. The front part gets distracted. It hears the noises around me, senses physical discomfort, and gets in the way of prayer. It lacks an off switch.

The back part is where God speaks to me, but it gets bullied by the front part. In order for the back to receive, the front needs to quiet down. The Rosary is perfect for this. While reciting Hail Marys, the front part of my mind stays busy enough to let the back reflect on the mysteries and open up space for God to enter. After five decades, my mind is quiet and calm.

If you're new to the Rosary, here are the prayers and mysteries. Words to the prayers are found in "Common Catholic Prayers."

- While holding the cross: Pray the Apostles' Creed.
- First bead: Pray the Our Father.
- First set of three beads: Pray three Hail Marys for an increase in the virtues of faith, hope, and charity.
- On the center bead or medal: Announce first mystery and recite the Our Father.
- On each bead of the first set of ten: Recite ten Hail Marys, one for each bead.
- After the Hail Marys, recite the Glory Be and the

Fatima prayer (usually holding onto the space between the Hail Mary beads and the next Our Father bead).

Repeat for each of the remaining four mysteries.

Conclude with Hail Holy Queen and the final Rosary prayer. (If your rosary has a medal or a large bead that connects the five decades to the cross, you can say the final prayers while holding this part.)

THE MYSTERIES

Joyful Mysteries (prayed on Mondays and Saturdays, and on Sundays during Advent)

1. The Annunciation
2. The Visitation
3. The Nativity
4. The Presentation in the Temple
5. The Finding in the Temple

Sorrowful Mysteries (prayed on Tuesdays and Fridays, and on Sundays during Lent)

1. The Agony in the Garden
2. The Scourging at the Pillar
3. The Crowning with Thorns
4. The Carrying of the Cross
5. The Crucifixion and Death

Glorious Mysteries (prayed on Wednesdays and Sundays outside of Advent and Lent)

1. The Resurrection
2. The Ascension
3. The Descent of the Holy Spirit
4. The Assumption
5. The Coronation of Mary

Luminous Mysteries (prayed on Thursdays)

1. The Baptism of Christ in the Jordan
2. The Wedding Feast at Cana
3. Jesus' Proclamation of the Kingdom of God

4. The Transfiguration
5. The Institution of the Eucharist

Pray the Rosary while you sit in adoration. If your mind gets distracted, gently bring yourself back. It is okay. It is a learning process.

The Memorare

We have a special gift in the Virgin Mary: She is a woman, fully human, who models for us how to follow Christ. As Jesus' first disciple, she accepted God's plan for her life despite the challenge of a virgin pregnancy. God trusted her so much that he came to earth as a baby completely dependent on her.

When Jesus was dying on the cross, and John and Mary stood before him, he gave Mary to John to be his mother, and John to Mary as her son:

> When Jesus saw his mother and the disciple there whom he loved, he said to his mother, "Woman, behold, your son." Then he said to the disciple, "Behold, your mother." And from that hour the disciple took her into his home. (John 19:26–27 [NABRE])

In these simple words, Jesus gave Mary to all of us as our mother. Just as God trusted her with his human life, we can trust her with our spiritual life, for her goal is simple: to lead others to Jesus. Mary's role has always been to point others to her son. We can be assured of her intercession when we ask for it.

Saint Bernard of Clairvaux is considered the author of the Memorare, a poetic prayer from the twelfth century that petitions the Blessed Virgin for help:

> Remember O most gracious Virgin Mary, that never was it known that anyone who fled to thy protection, implored thy help, or sought thine intercession was left unaided.
>
> Inspired by this confidence, I fly unto thee, O Virgin of virgins, my mother; to thee do I come, before thee I stand, sinful and sorrowful. O Mother of the Word Incarnate, despise not my petitions, but in thy mercy hear and answer me.

We know of Mary's love for us and her desire to intercede on our behalf. In times of darkness or trouble, when we cannot find the words to express our frustration, sadness, or despair, we can turn to the Memorare with confidence that Mary will have the words, and she will petition Jesus.

Mother Teresa often prayed the Memorare in what she called a Flying Novena. When she or her fellow sisters were in need of assistance but lacked time for a full-fledged nine-hour or nine-day novena, they turned to the Memorare. They prayed ten Memorares — nine for the novena proper and one in thanksgiving — so great was their confidence in the efficacy of the prayer.

Pray with John 19:26–27. Imagine you are the beloved disciple to whom Jesus is speaking. How can you relate to Mary as your spiritual mother? If you have issues with your earthly mother, this may be hard. Be patient and ask for guidance from Our Lord.

The Divine Mercy Chaplet

The Divine Mercy Chaplet comes to us from Saint Maria Faustina Kowalska, a Polish sister who received visits from Jesus. It is a prayer invoking God's mercy not just for us, but the world. It can be said using regular rosary beads at any time, but it is often recited at 3:00 p.m., in remembrance of Christ's death.

Here is how to pray the Divine Mercy Chaplet:

- On the cross of your rosary: You expired, Jesus, but the source of life gushed forth for souls, and the ocean of mercy opened up for the whole world. O Fount of Life, unfathomable Divine Mercy, envelop the whole world and empty yourself out upon us.
- O Blood and Water, which gushed forth from the heart of Jesus as a fount of Mercy for us, I trust in

You! (Repeat three times.)

- On the first three beads: Recite one Our Father, one Hail Mary, and the Apostles' Creed.

- For each decade of the chaplet, on the Our Father bead: Pray "Eternal Father, I offer you the Body and Blood, Soul and Divinity of your dearly beloved Son, our Lord Jesus Christ, in atonement for our sins and those of the whole world."

- On each Hail Mary bead: Pray "For the sake of his sorrowful passion, have mercy on us and on the whole world."

- Concluding prayers (these can be prayed while holding the center bead or medal of your rosary):

Holy God, Holy Mighty One, Holy Immortal One, have mercy on us and on the whole world. (Repeat three times.)

Eternal God, in whom mercy is endless and the treasury of compassion inexhaustible, look kindly upon us and increase your mercy in us, that in difficult moments we might not despair nor become despondent, but with great confidence submit ourselves to your holy will, which is Love and Mercy itself.

Novenas

Novenas are a uniquely Catholic way of praying. I learned about them as a child back when people believed that they needed to publish a thanksgiving for answered prayers in the newspaper. Our local Catholic paper often had a novena or two tucked between news articles.

I've since learned that the efficacy of novenas or any other form of prayer is not dependent on publication but rather the sincere desire of the one praying that God's will be done. The word *novena* comes from the Latin word for nine. The prayer is offered nine times, most often for nine consecutive days or hours, or simply said nine times in a row.

The novena is said to originate from the nine days between the Ascension of Jesus to heaven and Pentecost when Mary and the apostles stayed in the upper room. Father Jim White, a

Redemptorist priest, says, "Novenas aren't for controlling God, but for opening ourselves to God in order to increase our faith and grow in love of God and neighbor. Novenas are about inner healing, obtaining special graces, transformation, and growing in virtue and holiness."

There are many novenas available to us, from the Flying Novena said by Mother Teresa and her sisters, to novenas offered to saints requesting their intercession. There is a novena of confidence to the Sacred Heart, a Divine Mercy novena, a Christmas novena, a nine-day prayer for life, and many more. A Google search will bring up many options. There is even a website — praymorenovenas.com — where you can sign up to participate and a novena prayer is sent to your email inbox each morning.

Praying a novena is a beautiful way to practice persistence in prayer and unite yourself to a specific intention. We can be assured that if we offer it to Jesus and sincerely desire that his will be done, our prayer will be answered. The next time you have something or someone for whom you want to pray more deeply, consider a novena — and don't be shy about setting an alarm to help you remember. If you attend adoration weekly at a specific time, you could make that your time for praying the novena each day.

The Litany of Humility

Legend has it that this powerful prayer was written by Cardinal Rafael Merry del Val (1865–1930). It offers much to meditate on, so take it slowly:

O Jesus, meek and humble of heart, hear me.
From the desire of being esteemed, deliver me, Jesus.
From the desire of being loved, deliver me, Jesus.
From the desire of being extolled, deliver me, Jesus.
From the desire of being honored, deliver me, Jesus.
From the desire of being praised, deliver me, Jesus.
From the desire of being preferred to others, deliver me,
    Jesus.
From the desire of being consulted, deliver me, Jesus.
From the desire of being approved, deliver me, Jesus.

From the fear of being humiliated, deliver me, Jesus.
From the fear of being despised, deliver me, Jesus.
From the fear of suffering rebukes, deliver me, Jesus.
From the fear of being calumniated, deliver me, Jesus.
From the fear of being forgotten, deliver me, Jesus.
From the fear of being ridiculed, deliver me, Jesus.
From the fear of being wronged, deliver me, Jesus.
From the fear of being suspected, deliver me, Jesus.

That others may be loved more than I,
     Jesus, grant me the grace to desire it.
That others may be esteemed more than I,
     Jesus, grant me the grace to desire it.
That, in the opinion of the world, others may increase
and I may decrease,
     Jesus, grant me the grace to desire it.
That others may be chosen and I set aside,
     Jesus, grant me the grace to desire it.
That others may be praised and I go unnoticed,
     Jesus, grant me the grace to desire it.
That others may be preferred to me in everything,
     Jesus, grant me the grace to desire it.
That others may become holier than I, provided that I

may become as holy as I should be,
    Jesus, grant me the grace to desire it.

The Litany of Trust

By Sr. Faustina Maria Pio, Sister of Life:[†]

From the belief that I have to earn your love,
  Deliver me, Jesus.
From the fear that I am unlovable,
  Deliver me, Jesus.
From the false security that I have what it takes,
  Deliver me, Jesus.
From the fear that trusting you will leave me more destitute,
  Deliver me, Jesus.
From all suspicion of your words and promises,

---

† Reprinted with permission

Deliver me, Jesus.

From the rebellion against childlike dependency on you,
Deliver me, Jesus.

From refusals and reluctances in accepting your will,
Deliver me, Jesus.

From anxiety about the future,
Deliver me, Jesus.

From resentment or excessive preoccupation with the past,
Deliver me, Jesus.

From restless self-seeking in the present moment,
Deliver me, Jesus.

From disbelief in your love and presence,
Deliver me, Jesus.

From the fear of being asked to give more than I have,
Deliver me, Jesus.

From the belief that my life has no meaning or worth,
Deliver me, Jesus.

From the fear of what love demands,
Deliver me, Jesus.

From discouragement,
Deliver me, Jesus.

That you are continually holding me, sustaining me, loving me,

> Jesus, I trust in you.

That your love goes deeper than my sins and failings,

> Jesus, I trust in you.

That not knowing what tomorrow brings is an invitation to lean on you,

> Jesus, I trust in you.

That you are with me in my suffering,

> Jesus, I trust in you.

That my suffering, united to your own, will bear fruit in this life and the next,

> Jesus, I trust in you.

That you will not leave me orphan, that you are present in Your Church,

> Jesus, I trust in you.

That your plan is better than anything else,

> Jesus, I trust in you.

That you always hear me and in Your goodness always respond to me,

> Jesus, I trust in you.

That you give me the grace to accept forgiveness and to forgive others,

Jesus, I trust in you.
That you give me all the strength I need for what is asked,
Jesus, I trust in you.
That my life is a gift,
Jesus, I trust in you.
That you will teach me to trust You,
Jesus, I trust in you.
That You are my Lord and my God,
Jesus, I trust in you.
That I am your beloved one,
Jesus, I trust in you.

Amen.

Teach Me, Jesus

I desire to be empty of everything that isn't of you.

    Teach me, Jesus.

I desire to stop being concerned with me and be more concerned with you and others.

    Teach me, Jesus.

I desire to be in full communion with you.

    Teach me, Jesus.

I desire to rest in your gaze.

    Teach me, Jesus.

I desire to care more about how you see me, and less about how the world sees me.

    Teach me, Jesus.

I desire to be what you want me to be instead of what I want me to be.

Teach me, Jesus.
I desire to be a bridge to you for others, but only if that is your desire.
Teach me, Jesus.
I desire to radiate your love.
Teach me, Jesus.
I desire for others to see you in me, not me.
Teach me, Jesus.
I desire to embrace with joy your plan for my life, believing that it is sufficient.
Teach me, Jesus.
I desire to be satisfied with what you want from me, even and especially if it feels small and insignificant.
Teach me, Jesus.
I desire to desire the quiet where you reside.
Teach me, Jesus.

Lord, you loved me into being and your love keeps me alive. You know my weakness, my faults, my alarming littleness, yet you pursue me with passion. In your arms is unsurpassing peace, in your gaze is rest, in your heart is love I can only imagine. Teach me to run toward you with abandon, confident in your desire for me to be in communion with you. Amen.

Common Catholic Prayers

While God loves to hear the words of our hearts, sometimes we need other people's words. Here are some beautiful Catholic prayers that may be helpful while you're in adoration.

APOSTLES' CREED

I believe in God, the Father Almighty, Creator of Heaven and
. earth;
and in Jesus Christ, his only Son Our Lord,
Who was conceived by the Holy Spirit, born of the Virgin Mary,
suffered under Pontius Pilate, was crucified, died, and was
buried.
He descended into Hell; the third day he rose again from the dead;
He ascended into Heaven, and is seated at the right hand of God,
the Father almighty; from thence he shall come to judge the

living and the dead.
I believe in the Holy Spirit, the holy Catholic Church, the communion of saints, the forgiveness of sins, the resurrection of the body and life everlasting.
Amen.

OUR FATHER

Our Father, who art in heaven, hallowed be thy name. Thy kingdom come. Thy will be done, on earth as it is in heaven. Give us this day our daily bread, and forgive us our trespasses as we forgive those who trespass against us. And lead us not into temptation, but deliver us from evil. Amen.

HAIL MARY

Hail Mary, full of grace, the Lord is with thee. Blessed art thou among women, and blessed is the fruit of thy womb, Jesus. Holy Mary, mother of God, pray for us sinners now, and at the hour of our death. Amen.

GLORY BE (DOXOLOGY)

Glory be to the Father, and to the Son, and to the Holy Spirit. As it was in the beginning, is now, and ever shall be, world without end. Amen.

FATIMA PRAYER

O my Jesus, forgive us our sins, save us from the fires of hell, and lead all souls to heaven, especially those who are in most need of thy mercy.

ANIMA CHRISTI

By Saint Ignatius of Loyola

Soul of Christ, sanctify me. Body of Christ, save me. Blood of Christ, inebriate me. Water from the side of Christ, wash me. Passion of Christ, strengthen me. O good Jesus, hear me. Within thy wounds hide me. Separated from thee let me never be. From the malignant enemy, defend me. At the hour of death, call me. And close to thee bid me. That with thy saints I may be praising thee, forever and ever. Amen.

SAINT PATRICK'S BREASTPLATE PRAYER

I arise today
Through a mighty strength, the invocation of the Trinity,
Through a belief in the Threeness,
Through confession of the Oneness
Of the Creator of creation.
I arise today
Through the strength of Christ's birth and his baptism,

Through the strength of his crucifixion and his burial,
Through the strength of his resurrection and His ascension,
Through the strength of his descent for the judgment of doom.
I arise today
Through the strength of the love of cherubim,
In obedience of angels,
In service of archangels,
In the hope of resurrection to meet with reward,
In the prayers of patriarchs,
In preachings of the apostles,
In faiths of confessors,
In innocence of virgins,
In deeds of righteous men.
I arise today
Through the strength of heaven;
Light of the sun,
Splendor of fire,
Speed of lightning,
Swiftness of the wind,
Depth of the sea,
Stability of the earth,
Firmness of the rock.
I arise today

Through God's strength to pilot me;
God's might to uphold me,
God's wisdom to guide me,
God's eye to look before me,
God's ear to hear me,
God's word to speak for me,
God's hand to guard me,
God's way to lie before me,
God's shield to protect me,
God's hosts to save me
From snares of the devil,
From temptations of vices,
From everyone who desires me ill,
Afar and anear,
Alone or in a multitude.
I summon today all these powers between me and evil,
Against every cruel merciless power that opposes my body and
 soul,
Against incantations of false prophets,
Against black laws of pagandom,
Against false laws of heretics,
Against craft of idolatry,
Against spells of women and smiths and wizards,

Against every knowledge that corrupts man's body and soul.
Christ shield me today
Against poison, against burning,
Against drowning, against wounding,
So that reward may come to me in abundance.
Christ with me, Christ before me, Christ behind me,
Christ in me, Christ beneath me, Christ above me,
Christ on my right, Christ on my left,
Christ when I lie down, Christ when I sit down,
Christ in the heart of every man who thinks of me,
Christ in the mouth of every man who speaks of me,
Christ in the eye that sees me,
Christ in the ear that hears me.
I arise today
Through a mighty strength, the invocation of the Trinity,
Through a belief in the Threeness,
Through a confession of the Oneness
Of the Creator of creation.

SAINT MICHAEL'S PRAYER

Saint Michael the Archangel, defend us in battle. Be our protection against the wickedness and snares of the Devil. May God rebuke him, we humbly pray, and do thou, O Prince of the heavenly hosts, by the power of God, cast into hell Satan, and all the evil spirits, who prowl about the world seeking the ruin of souls. Amen.

JESUS PRAYER

Lord Jesus Christ, Son of the living God, have mercy on me, a sinner.

BAPTISMAL PROMISES

Do you reject Satan?
R. I do.

And all his works?
R. I do.

And all his empty promises?
R. I do.

Do you believe in God, the Father Almighty, Creator of heaven and earth?

R. I do.

Do you believe in Jesus Christ, his only Son, our Lord, who was born of the Virgin Mary, was crucified, died, and was buried, rose from the dead, and is now seated at the right hand of the Father?
R. I do.

Do you believe in the Holy Spirit, the holy Catholic church, the communion of saints, the forgiveness of sins, the resurrection of the body, and life everlasting?
R. I do.

GUARDIAN ANGEL PRAYER
Angel of God, my guardian dear,
To whom God's love commits me here.
Ever this day be at my side
To light and guard, to rule and guide. Amen.

ANGELUS
This prayer is traditionally said at 6 a.m., noon, and/or 6 pm.

The Angel of the Lord declared to Mary: and she conceived of the Holy Spirit.

Hail Mary, full of grace, the Lord is with thee, blessed art thou among women and blessed is the fruit of thy womb, Jesus. Holy Mary, Mother of God, pray for us sinners, now and at the hour of our death. Amen.

Behold I am the handmaid of the Lord: Be it done unto me according to thy word.

Hail Mary …

And the Word became Flesh: and dwelt among us.

Hail Mary …

Pray for us, O Holy Mother of God, that we may be made worthy of the promises of Christ.

Let us pray: Pour forth, we beseech thee, O Lord, thy grace into our hearts; that we, to whom the Incarnation of Christ, thy Son, was made known by the message of an angel, may by his passion and cross be brought to the glory of His Resurrection, through the same Christ Our Lord. Amen.

BOOKS THAT ARE GREAT TO READ IN ADORATION

The Story of a Soul — Saint Thérèse of Lisieux
Divine Mercy in My Soul: Diary of St. Maria Faustina Kowalska
He Leadeth Me — Walter Ciszek, SJ
I Believe in Love — Fr. Jean C. J. D'Elbee
Come Be My Light — Mother Teresa
The Great Divorce — C. S. Lewis
The Screwtape Letters — C. S. Lewis
The Real Story — Edward Sri and Curtis Martin
The World's First Love: Mary, Mother of God — Ven. Fulton Sheen
A School of Prayer — Pope Benedict XVI

By Father Jacques Philippe

Searching for and Maintaining Peace
Time for God
In the School of the Holy Spirit

Conclusion

My hope is that you have developed a regular practice of Eucharistic adoration. I pray that you have experienced the fruits that come from a rich and consistent prayer life — that you know you are deeply and powerfully loved by Jesus who desires only beauty and goodness for you; that his grace is spilling into your heart; and that you feel more inner joy and peace. I hope you are becoming better at quieting down and hearing God's voice. He has much to share with you.

I also hope you have begun to face some stumbling blocks to prayer and brought them to Jesus, knowing his love is big and unconditional. I hope you are able to push aside the lies that you are unseen, unknown, unworthy, or unlovable, because in Jesus' eyes you are none of those things.

Jesus sees you.

He knows you.
He values you.
And he loves you.

My prayer is that book has helped you begin a journey closer to Jesus. Thank you for reading this book. It was my honor to write it.

Acknowledgments

Thank you, Mary Beth, for believing in me as a writer and giving me this opportunity.

Thank you, Margaret, for discipling me when you had a lot of other stuff to do.

Thank you, Amy, for reading this book while it was still in its infancy and therefore not very good.

Most importantly, thank you, God, for giving me life and giving all of us your Son.

All glory be to the Father, and to the Son, and to the Holy Spirit, as it was in the beginning, is now, and ever shall be, world without end. Amen.

About the Author

Merridith Frediani loves words and is delighted by good sentences. She also loves Lake Michigan, dahlias, the first sip of hot coffee in the morning, millennials, and playing Sheepshead with her husband and three kids. She works for the Archdiocese of Milwaukee in the New Evangelization office and writes for CatholicMom.com, Ascension Press, Diocesan.com, and her local *Catholic Herald*. This is her first book.